# *GIRL DAD*

CHERYL BARTON

Published by: Cheryl Barton Publishing, LLC

This book is a work of fiction and any references or similarities to actual events, real people, living or dead, or to real places, are intended to give the novel a sense of reality. Any similarities in names, characters, places and incidents is entirely coincidental.



For printing and/or copying permission requests, write to the publisher, addressed to:
"Attention: Permissions Coordinator," at the address below.

Cheryl Barton Publishing, LLC
P.O. Box 962
Reisterstown, Maryland 21136
www.crbarton.com
or
Email: prez@crbarton.com

Ordering Information:
Quantity sales.
Special discounts are available on quantity purchases by corporations, associations, and others. For details, contact the publisher at the address above.

Orders by U.S. trade bookstores and wholesalers.
Please contact prez@crbarton.com



**ISBN-13: 978-1-948950-20-6**

# ***Dedication***

To my very own #GirlDad, my father, John Barton, Jr., the perfect example of the kind of dad every girl should have. My life has been filled with so much love and support from the world's best dad. I always claim that my love for reading came from you.

I remember growing up and watching you read one book after another and sometimes, I'd smile when I saw you reading more than one book at a time. I developed that habit as well. It just works for us avid readers!

Daddy, thank you for letting me see, know and feel what the love of a dad is supposed to be. Your unconditional love has given me an experience that not every girl gets to have. I am a daddy's girl, something I've always said and what I am most proud of is that you're *MY* #GirlDad. We're in this together.

I love you, I adore being your daughter and I thank God for deciding my life would be most blessed with you as my father. Thank you for being you, for introducing me to reading and most of all for bringing Maryland steamed crabs into my life (smile).

I love you, Daddy

*Cheryl*

**ALSO BY CHERYL BARTON on**
**WWW.CHERYLBARTON.NET**

**Bachelor Series**
Bachelor Not for Sale
A Designed Affair
A Perfect Combination
Love at Last

**Amorous Occupations Series**
The Artist
The Bookkeeper
The Chef
The Dancer
The Electrician

**A Lovers' Heart Series**
Heartthrob
Heartbeat
Heartbreaker

**Brothers of Chi-Town Series**
I Can't Let Go
Swagger and Baggage
Claiming His Child
Always Bet on Black
*It Takes Two to Tangle – July 2020 Release*

**Malibu Hearts Series**
And Then There Was You

**Stand Alone Romance Novels**
Snowbound
Cupid's Arrow

One Wish
His Halloween Promise
Home for Thanksgiving
Holly for Christmas
A Better Man
Bossy
Un-Break My Heart
Love on Top
Take a Knee
Love at First Sight
My First Love
Black Love
A Younger Man
The Lake House
True Lies or True Love
When I Think of You

**Inspirational Romance**

Down, But Not Out: Breaking Chains
She Said No

**Inspirational**

A Letter to My Mother
Rescue Me
Release Me
*Restore Me – October 2020 Release*
*Save Me – February 2021 Release*

**Scandalous/Drama Novels**

**Divas of High Hill Series**

*Secrets, Book 1 – August 2020 Release*

## ***Acknowledgement***

Before the death of Kobe Bryant, I admit that I'd never heard the term, "Girl Dad".   On January 26, 2020, Kobe Bryant and his daughter, Gianna Bryant died in a helicopter accident in California and on that day, the world paused. Shock was heard and felt around the world at the loss of a man many considered an icon on the basketball court. After the accident, many were able to experience, through old video clips and photos, that Kobe was much more than that. I'm not speaking about his business and endorsements, but I'm acknowledging his unfailing love  and devotion to his four daughters, the youngest only months old at the time of his death. During an interview on a late-night television show, Kobe explained how proud he was to be a  "Girl Dad" when people constantly ask if he was disappointed that he didn't have a son. He proudly boasted that he was happy about his four daughters and the way he spoke of them, you had no doubt that he adored them and never questioned not having a son. It's possible that if his life had been longer, he and his wife may have had other children and may have even had a son, but even that would never have diminished the deep-rooted love he has for his daughters. I connected to his feelings and I mourned with the rest of the world, not just because he and his daughter died, but his three other daughters will miss the great father he would have continued to be to them. I fell in love with the term , "Girl Dad" and I knew right away that as a writer, I was going to write a book about a father's love for his daughter. This isn't a book about Kobe Bryant or his daughters, but I'm thankful that his undying love for them inspired me to write this book. I hope you enjoy Cyrus and Shiloh's story and that you'll fall in love with this "Girl Dad" and his daughter.

Be inspired and celebrate the "Girl Dad" in your life.

# 1

Daniella Rice tried to stifle another yawn as her supervisor, Teresa Wallace, walked by her desk. To her dismay, the yawn found its way out of her mouth even as she used her bring pink-tipped painted fingers to try and hold her mouth shut. This was, by far, the largest of the twenty or so yawns she'd released since arriving at the Virginia Social Services office where she has worked for the past five years as a social worker in the infant and children's division. When Teresa caught her mid-yawn and smiled her way, Daniella waved and tried to smile with an apologetic look. This wasn't the first time she'd been caught at work showing how little sleep she'd gotten and she knew it wouldn't be her last. Luckily, Teresa knew the reason, having experienced herself many nights of no sleep and so an explanation wasn't necessary.

"Late night?" Teresa asked.

Daniella pressed the palms of her hands on the

edge of her redwood desk and pushed until her chair turned in Teresa's direction. When her hands slipped slightly, she rubbed them feverishly across the navy-blue dress pants of the two-piece suit she pulled out of her closet this morning after only a few hours of sleep and was happy that it was one that didn't need ironing. If it had, she would have been apologizing all day for her unkempt and disheveled look, the pains of a social worker who got a call in the middle of the night that a five-year old child had been left deserted at the local police department.

"I swear that the nights when I'm on call, I get the one's that happen in the middle of the night. Do you have a moment for me to brief you on what happened?" Daniella asked, standing from her ratted old black leather desk chair that had seen better days.

"Uh, sure. I have some time before the morning staff meeting. Come on in my office," Teresa said as she turned and walked away.

Daniella started to follow her and then reached back to her desk for the file folder on the little girl she was sent to see after. Grabbing the folder, she checked it to be sure her notes were inside. Seeing them, she quickened her steps to catch up to Teresa as she entered her glass enclosed office at the end of the long, black rubber mat that covered the walkway which led from one end of the third floor of their office building to the other. Stumbling slightly, she caught her balance just as she reached the office door.

She silently cursed herself for putting on high heels when what she should have done was kept on the sneakers she'd worn to the office. This was her day in the office and not out in the field, so she knew she would have been able to get away with not wearing shoes and besides, Friday's were usually days where they could dress down a little.

The minute she finished bringing Teresa up to date on the events of the night before, her next act of the day would be to change out of her heels and rock the new Jordan's she kept in the locked cabinet on the side of her desk. She'd worn New Balance sneakers to work, but today felt like a Michael Jordan sneaker kind of day.

"How was your night?" Daniella asked, sitting in one of the two brown, wrought iron office side chairs with worn leather seating. She wondered how many people shouted in their heads at how uncomfortable the chair was, yet refrained from expressing that opinion to Teresa.

"It was good. My husband and I finally got the chance to have dinner at home together. It's been a while since our schedules have been open at the same time and last night, when you agreed to be on-call, I went home and cooked a meal fit for a king of rib-eye steaks, grilled Cajun shrimp, sautéed broccoli and cauliflower and I even put an apple pie in the oven which we ate right out of the tin in front of the television in our family room. We will have our grandkids this weekend, so it was good to have some quiet time before the storm when they are dropped off by my daughter and my son after the kids get out of school," Teresa joked.

"All six of them?" Daniella asked.

When Teresa laughed out loud, Daniella laughed with her, knowing how much she loved her grandkids, but also imagining that at sixty-two, her six grandkids, all under the age of twelve, could be a handful.

"Yes, all six. My kids are double dating with their spouses to a concert and we're giving them a weekend free of the mayhem that usually occurs at their houses with three kids each. It will be me yawning on Monday instead of you," Teresa joked.

Daniella laughed even harder, feeling her entire body join in on the jovial exchange. The running joke in the office was not about those who spent the day yawning, but of those who did not – a signal that they didn't have enough work to do or enough cases that kept them up at night like her case the night before did, or rather early this morning.

"Yeah, the call last night ended up lasting the entire night and it was a night of little sleep and lots of yawns," Daniella admitted.

"Why didn't you take the day off or at least come in later? You know I always approve the time when you end up with an all-nighter. It would have been okay," Teresa offered.

"I know, but I wanted to get right on this one

today. You should have seen this little girl from last night."

When Teresa looked at her over the top of the glasses that were already sliding down her nose, Daniella knew what she was thinking.

"You can't take them all home, Dani. I know you want to and you have a big, gigantic heart of gold filled with compassion for every child that comes across our doors, but you can't get so involved that year heart yearns to make the world right for all of them at one and remember about emotional distancing. I know it's hard, but we stand in the gap for these children – we don't take on the burdens that comes with what happens to them. We fix what we can."

Daniella huffed silently, knowing the short speech was coming. Teresa knew she'd hired a staff that was strong when it came to dealing with what plagued the youngest victims in Richmond, Virginia, but her staff also wanted to fix the problems of the world so that no child would have to endure a life of loneliness or abuse, something they encountered every day.

"I know and I tried. I didn't take her home. There was a bed for her at one of our favorite foster homes and when I called Ms. Rose a few hours ago, she was waiting on her porch for me at four this morning, bless her heart," Daniella said as she looked down and began flipping through her folder.

She let her eyes drift away from Teresa who she

knew would see that leaving the little girl was again a struggle, but Daniella was learning every day to separate her personal feelings from her work life. She had to keep fighting to do that if she were going to make it in the world of looking after the welfare of a child.

"Okay, bring me up to date. What kept you up all night?" Teresa inquired.

Daniella shifted to a comfortable position and then dived in.

"Well, I got a call from the police department around eleven last night about a five-year-old little girl who had been dropped off there by a woman."

"By a parent?" Teresa asked.

Daniella leaned forward, almost dropping the folder to the floor and anxious to get the story out, but knowing she needed to give Teresa the full background.

"No. Okay, let me go back a little bit. Do you remember the police chase last week where a man and a woman were speeding away from the police after the man shot up a drug corner? During the chase, he lost control of the car and it careened off of the road and over an embankment. It took the police an entire day to get the bodies out of the car because of how it rested on the side of a mountain."

Daniella leaned back and searched through her notes for the names.

"I do remember that," Teresa said.

"The woman was twenty-eight-year-old Brenda Johnson. The man was forty-year-old, Shelton Monroe. According the report I received from the police, they both had priors and Shelton actually had a warrant out for his arrest on several charges from drug possession and drug distribution to assault, theft and burglary. Miss Johnson had a record of charges that stemmed from drug possession, drug use, as well as theft and prostitution," Daniella explained.

"Was the child in the car?" Teresa inquired.

"No. She had been with a friend of Ms. Johnson and that same friend is who dropped her off at the police station because she didn't know what to do with her."

"Okay, it's a blessing that she wasn't in the car."

Daniella nodded in agreement.

"The child is five-year-old Shiloh Antonia Johnson. According to the friend, she is Miss Johnson's daughter, but not the daughter of Shelton Monroe. Sometime before that chase, Shiloh had been left with this family friend, whose name is Jasmine Duran. According to her, she was asked to watch Shiloh while Miss Johnson went out with Mr. Monroe. That was the last she saw them until someone told her about the crash."

"She wasn't told by the police?" Teresa asked.

"No. According to them, they had no idea where the two people in the car lived. The car they were in was a stolen car and the identification on both of them did not lead to the place where they were now living. If Jasmine had not come into the police station last night with Shiloh, they wouldn't know where the pair lived. She showed up because after waiting a few days after hearing about their deaths, she realized she was left with Shiloh and didn't know what to do with her. After questioning her, the police had to let her go because they had nothing on her. She gave them the address where Ms. Johnson lived and the police went to that house, but no one was there. According to the neighbors, the two lived there with the little girl for the past month or so. It appears that they moved around a lot. The police were able to locate family for Shelton, but no luck when it came to Brenda Johnson. They reached the father of Shelton Monroe, but he had no idea who Brenda was and he hadn't seen his son in years and so he was no help in locating any of her family," Daniella explained.

"So little Shiloh is the latest orphan to come through our doors. There is no family at all and no way to find any?" Teresa asked.

"It may take some time, but right now, none. Jasmine said all she knew was that Brenda never talked about her family. She left home when she was about fifteen and lived from house to house with friends. She said Brenda was from somewhere on the west coast, but wasn't sure where. She knew that years ago, Brenda showed up in Virginia after some time in D.C. and possibly New York. There is literally nothing as far as where this girl came from and so Shiloh is alone and yes, that means, she's an orphan. There is one thing Jasmine was able to tell the police. Apparently, as I stated, Shelton Monroe is not the child's biological father, but she knew that the birth father is a man named Cyrus Jackson who lives in Washington, D.C. and apparently runs some kind of club or something. I will say that after a quick check on who he may be, the police were able to find a record on him, if he's the correct Cyrus Jackson. He's been on their radar for some time because of allegations of illegal drug and money laundering activities. He apparently owns two night-clubs, several supermarkets, an apartment building, a recording studio and he has an office building where he's launching some kind of entertainment company, but has never sought any kind of bank financing which only means one thing," Daniella suggested as she looked over at Teresa without saying the words.

"Drug money," Teresa said.

Daniella nodded.

"If this is him, he does have a history that goes back to his juvenile years where those files are sealed. He has enough of a record as an adult that's frightening enough. Jasmine told the police about the clubs, which is all she knew about because Brenda Johnson told her that much. The other businesses they were able to find out about through sources at the D.C. Police Department."

"Whew. This little girl sure does have some colorful parents, that is if this man, Cyrus, is her father," Teresa suggested.

"True. Anyway, the police found some information on Shiloh at the house, including her birth certificate where Cyrus Jackson is listed as the father. They're not sure what he does or doesn't know about Shiloh, but I'll get some people on it this morning and we'll reach to him along with the local D.C. police to see if he acknowledges he's Shiloh's father. So far, there is no record of any child support payments or any public assistance given to Brenda Johnson for her and her daughter and I'll assume the life she was living with Shelton Monroe is how they survived," Daniella said, reading from her notes in the folder. She'd spent the rest of the night jotting down ideas and thoughts about the case, most were unfounded, but she liked to think about cases from all angles.

"Hmm. Cyrus Jackson, if he is the father, may not be the best option, but if he's family, he's family. It's at least a place to start," Teresa said.

"True. The police gave me some other information and I'm going through it all this morning before I reach to the D.C. Department of Child Services to ask for their help with Cyrus Jackson in notifying him. In the meantime, Ms. Rose has taken Shiloh in and we'll help her get the little girl enrolled in school as early as tomorrow. According to her birth certificate, with her age and her birthday, she should be in the kindergarten. We'll check local schools to see if she was enrolled anyplace. There's a lot to do and I know we don't like for children to stay in foster care if they have family, whether it be this Cyrus Jackson guy or if we are able to locate any of Shiloh's mother's family. I'll keep you posted," Daniella said, standing when she saw Teresa check the time. They were getting close to the start of the weekly staff meeting to wrap up the week.

"Okay, I want you to brief everyone at the staff meeting today and let's get you extra help if you need it. I want to know if this Cyrus Jackson person is her father and if he knows of any family for Shiloh's mother. Let's do all we can to find some family."

Daniella kept her head in her folder, looking from one document to the other, flipping page after page.

"Right," she muttered under her breath, unfocused on the conversation. Her mind was wandering to the frail little girl with the long, black, thick braids in old, dirty denim jeans and a white t-shirt that she could tell had been the little girl's outfit for quite a few days. She scanned the photos that the police had taken of Shiloh after she arrived at the police department. They were going to use them to ask the public if anyone was related to the little girl. They had to start somewhere. The saving grace was that she knew Ms. Rose would fix Shiloh up, get her a bath, get her hair washed and get her some fresh, clean clothes. She was appreciative of people like her who had a heart for children.

"What's wrong, Dani?" Teresa asked.

Exhaling, Daniella looked over and locked eyes with her.

"You should have seen this little girl. She was terrified, but you know what stood out the most?" she asked.

"What?" Teresa inquired.

"She never asked for her mother. Jasmine even said that Shiloh never asked why her mother hadn't come back for her. She didn't ask about Shelton Monroe. According to her, the only words she actually spoke were to say she was hungry or had to go to the bathroom. When I left the police station with her and I took her by the hand, she held my hand so tight, it was actually a little numb. When we got in my car and I strapped her into the car seat I stopped by the office to pick up on my way there, she never took her eyes off of me. She didn't look around – not out the window, nowhere, just at me," she explained.

"Sounds like she was terrified as most children left alone like that are, especially around a station filled with police," Teresa said.

"If I asked her a question, she wouldn't answer. When I took her to Ms. Rose, she was afraid to let go of my hand. You know how I get and this one just got to me. I kept wondering, why wasn't she missing her mother? When I asked the police about the house they went to check out, they told me it wasn't fit for an animal to live in, let alone people, especially a little girl. In what was her room, there was a single, dirty mattress on the floor, no bed, no dresser or anything. The other bedroom was just as bad with a dirty mattress, clothes and food scattered about. They found some clothes for her in black trash bags, but they didn't bring them because there were mice, roaches and every kind of critter running around. Other than the papers they were able to locate, they didn't take anything else. According to them, nothing was worth taking."

"Had this Jasmine been staying at this place with Shiloh this past week since the crash?" Teresa asked.

"No. She has an apartment where she lives with her own kids. After she heard about what happened, she waited a few days and then took her to the police. She said Shiloh had on the same clothes the whole time. Her kids are older and she didn't have anything for Shiloh to put on. I won't even get into that and how this child looked. That woman could have given her something or at least, a bath. Anyway, moving beyond that, I know it's time for the staff meeting. I'll brief on this case and another one I'm working on. I will need some help with Shiloh's case."

"As I mentioned before, it sounds like he may not be much better for this little girl, but let's see what happens. Either way, she'll be in the system for a while until it all gets worked out. Find out if we can get Ms. Rose some funds a little faster than our system usually allows and off the record, see if she needs anything and take it from our office fund."

Daniella shook her head acknowledging the subtle words. The state of Virginia and the city of Richmond did what they could with what they had, but she was happy that she worked in an office where everyone on staff dropped a few dollars here and there into a jar and when needed, they took from it to supplement those who, out of the kindness of their hearts, took in children who had no place else to go.

When Teresa stood and came around her desk, grabbing her folder for the staff meeting, Daniella was about to follow behind her when Teresa stopped and turned toward her, placing a hand softly on her shoulder. Daniella could read her eyes and knew what the questioning look was all about.

"I'm distancing," Daniella admitted, more to herself than to Teresa.

"I know and it's okay if it takes a while. Don't forget to do the job ahead of you. Shiloh will be just fine with Ms. Rose until we find family, even if it's Cyrus Jackson."

Daniella smiled slightly and nodded her head. From what the police were able to provide for her about Cyrus Jackson, he may end up being her father, but from his history, she had a feeling Shiloh could end up going from bad to worse. Only time would tell.

# 2

Cyrus Jackson sat behind the large black marble-topped desk in his third-floor office overlooking the dance floor of one of his two night-clubs, *Club CyEmp*, the hottest spot in Washington, D.C. for the young and sexy to hang out. His second location, *Club CyEmpTwo*, he knew was just as popular and catered to a slightly older, grown and sexy, yet still ready to party crowd, located a few miles away. Lights flashed, music blared, drinks were being poured and bought and money flowed easily for what he knew would be a hot night of partying as was every single Friday night that the club was open. A few years ago, he'd taken over ownership of the buildings which were clubs under two different owners where he strong-armed them into selling their buildings for a lot less than what they were worth, but they knew the other option didn't mean they would live to make another dollar if they didn't agree. Before he became a more business-oriented businessman, that was how he got what he wanted out of people

"The line outside to get in is three blocks long and we're already at capacity," Jason Scott, his number one, right-hand man shouted as he rubbed his hands together as if the money coming in was all his.

Cyrus allowed Jason to have a small part of the profits, but not enough for him to be this excited. He laughed at his antics.

"Did you tell them about *CyEmpTwo* that may have some room? I doubt if any of them will get in tonight. It's ladies' night and no one is leaving out any time soon. Have you seen the level of hotness and sexiness that's up in here tonight?" Cyrus asked as he leaned back comfortably in his leather office chair, placing his black, leather Gucci loafers up on the top of his desk, crossing his legs at the ankles as he lit up his second blunt of the night.

"We did and then I checked with that location and they are completely booked already too and it's not even midnight yet. No one left because they all want to be in here tonight. At least the crowd out there is tame and there are no issues that would call for the police to pay us a visit tonight," Jason said.

Cyrus looked at him sideways as he inhaled and held it a few seconds before blowing it out.

"We should never have a police problem again. Their pockets are a little fatter than usual tonight, so don't expect much by way of police interference. We can even let a few extras in and we'll be all good. Have you heard from Oscar tonight? I'm expecting a drop-off of a large load of money to clean and get back out on the streets. He was going to holla when his guys were on their way," Cyrus said.

For a split second, Cyrus wanted to outwardly show his own excitement over the idea of the amount of money he was about to make, though it is of an illegal nature, he was still rolling in it and was seeing the number of zeros of his cash on-hand expand. He was more than the small street hustler he'd been when he first got in the game years ago. He was a force and no one came at him who was ever able to brag about doing so. He didn't know of a dude that bold who didn't know the consequences of stepping to Cyrus Jackson.

"Uh, yeah, they are on the way. I got Little in the back along with Rock and Case. They're waiting on them and the duffle bags we're sending back are packed and ready to be handed off. The house over east is being counted out tonight and that handoff is set for tomorrow. We're all good, bro," Jason said.

"Get to Woody at the bank and tell him I'm coming through tomorrow and get a brick together for him," Cyrus said, giving an instruction he knew would be followed. Woody was a bank branch manager who made sure that all the money Cyrus brought to his bank was safe but not on any bank records. Even with his legitimate businesses, like his grocery stores and the apartment building he owned, there was no way he would be able to account for the amount of money he brought in which has made him a very rich man. He was richer than even his wildest dreams could have foreseen. Having a lot of money didn't make him a stupid man. He may not have all the book smarts others had, but he was street smart and now, business smart. He knew what to do to keep from ending up in jail ever again, a path from his past he would like to forget about.

He didn't live the life of a rich man, at least not yet because he knew he needed to live under the radar, but he still kept his eyes on every cent going out and coming in, especially the illegal money he filtered through his clubs and turned into clean, legit money on the streets and in his own stash.

"I'm on it, boss man. Listen, Stacie is signaling from below, asking if she can come up," Jason said.

Cyrus huffed with impatience. He liked Stacie, but she was having a hard time understanding that when he wanted her, he would send for her. He hated that she took liberties because she spread eagle for him whenever he wanted her to. That did not make for a relationship between them, but she was acting like it and he wasn't happy about it.

"No, she can't and go down and tell her to back it up a few steps and if she doesn't, she's having her last night in the club," Cyrus warned. "Oh, and while you're doing that, see if KC is down there. Bring that fool up here to answer for my missing money, but don't tell him what he's coming up here for. I can't get why people think because they are close to me and I lend them money that they don't have to pay it back on-time. Bring Bruno back with you for leverage in getting the truth," Cyrus added.

Bruno was his muscle to help him keep his own hands clean. Back before he learned to do business better, his hands had experiences with inflicting harm on those who wronged him and if not with his hands, then with one of the many weapons he owned that were in his arsenal. He was not to be tested or played with. It was important to him that anyone he encountered respected him or they would be dealt with. Luckily, he had enough guys in his crew now that he didn't have to deal with anyone directly. He put his guys to work.

"I got you," Jason said and left the office.

Cyrus stood and walked over to the wall of glass that allowed him to see the entire club from this spot. Looking out over the throngs of people bumping and grinding and spending money on expensive liquor, he felt on top of the world. He watched as Jason walked over to Stacie, his bed-bunny and her friends and gave her his message. He knew the moment she realized the consequences of pissing him off. When she didn't look his way, but instead turned to her girls and then they all walked toward the VIP area, he knew his message was clear.

Later, after the club closed, he already knew he would make his way to her place to have her show him how she can work her hips. Watching the sway of her hips and her large, round, shapely behind as she walked had him imagining all the things she could do with that body that gave him satisfaction. She may not be looking his way, but she knew he was watching her and he laughed out loud as she gave an extra wiggle as she walked. She knew what she was doing and he looked forward to reaping the benefits at the end of the night.

Stacie had a talent he loved, especially in the bedroom, but right now, his mind was on money and getting Oscar's men in and out without any problem. Oscar was his biggest partner in the drug game and they had made each other very rich. Like him, Oscar, who was out of New York, wasn't a man to be played with, but they had developed a mutual respect over the years that kept the violence between their groups to a minimum. In all, Cyrus applauded himself for how powerful he'd become and his power showed in how people reacted to him, men and women.

Looking around the room below after taking his eyes off of Stacie, he saw Kimberly, another of his sexy women who was already making him second guess his decision to pay Stacie a visit later. Kimberly did look his way, though she couldn't see him through the one-way glass, allowing him to see out, but no one could look up and see him. When she licked her lips and winked while running one manicured nail up the side of her arm, he knew what she had in mind. He was thinking that she may be invited up to his office before the night was over. He loved being him. He'd spent the night before with her and was looking for a repeat of their amorous night. When she winked at him again, though she couldn't see him, he winked back because he got the message. As she turned around and showed him her backside, he laughed because like most women, he knew that she believed she had him hooked on the booty, but little did she know that booty flowed as often as his money and he spotted quite a few other options in his club. He let her have her moment, only turning away from her when the door to his office opened and KC stumbled in, not by accident, but most likely because Bruno, who was close behind him, had pushed him in.

"KC!" Cyrus shouted, rubbing his hands together as he moved to sit on the leather sofa that lined the glass wall in his office.

"Boss. You wanted to see me?" KC asked, turning to Bruno who stood right behind him. After Jason entered, Cyrus heard him lock the office door. KC had heard that lock click also and Cyrus saw the look on his face that said it was clear that he wasn't going anywhere.

"I did. Any idea why I called you in here tonight?" Cyrus asked.

"Uh, n...n...no," KC stuttered out, looking around

the office at all three men.

"Really? You don't have a clue?" Cyrus asked.

"I don't know, Boss. Jason said you wanted to see me, but he didn't say why," KC offered, shaking nervously from one foot to the other.

Cyrus liked to incite fear into those who cross him. They needed to know what would happen when they did in order to not have a repeat occurrence.

"Again, really? Do you know who you're talking to? I don't call you guys in here for no reason at all. There's always a reason and this isn't a good one. We are not about to have a kumbaya moment. I don't have all night, so let's get down to it. This is about ten grand that you seem to have forgotten you needed to pay back. I don't give money away as gifts – that was a loan and the due date was a month ago which not only means you're late, but it also means you owe me another ten grand on top of that. I'm not a bank and when I loan you something, I expect it back or Bruno will pay you a visit. Luckily, he's here, you're here and we can take care of this right now. You know I don't play about my money," Cyrus explained as he stood and walked over until he stood right in front of KC, who he could tell was no shivering uncontrollably with warranted nervousness.

Towering over KC, who stood at well under six feet, while he himself stood at six-feet-four, Cyrus grimaced and tried to hold back his rage. At thirty-two, he's spent his time beating guys down, stealing their pride in the process and tonight, he felt the need to release a little rage and send a reminder of who he was, something KC has clearly forgotten.

Before KC could ascertain what was coming, Cyrus slammed his fist into KC's gut and watched as the man crumpled to the floor, gasping for air and groaning.

"I'm sorry, Boss," KC groaned out in pain. "I'll get your money. I promise I will get it."

For good measure, Cyrus kicked him in the gut with all the power he could muster in his leg and this time KC rolled around on the floor, trying to scutter away like an animal running in fear. Before he could get too far, Bruno picked him up by his collar and stood him up to this full height, holding on to him to be sure he didn't get away. KC tried to slump to the floor, but Bruno held him in place.

"Boss, let me do this," Bruno exclaimed. "I'll take care of it," he added.

"Nah, I got this. Where's my money, KC? What did you do with it, huh?" Cyrus asked getting right up in his face.

"I..I..gave it to my sister to pay for my niece's hospital bill. She had to use her rent money to cover the bill and was falling behind. I promise I'll get your money back. I'll go right out and make it now and get you your money. I have most of it, but not all of it. I as planning to make it by staying out all night tonight. The corners are hot tonight and I promise I'll have it, boss," KC explain, still struggling to catch his breath.

Cyrus was about to hit him again and then he remembered the niece that had to have surgery a few weeks ago. At least he knew that KC wasn't lying to him. Backing up, Cyrus stretched and cracked the kink in his neck. He straightened up the black button-down shirt and black slacks he was wearing.

"I want my money and because I know about the situation with your niece, which I forgot about, I'll give you a little break. I'll do away with the extra interest and give you a month to get it back to me. Next time, don't make me have to come to you about something you owe me. You come straight to me and let me know what's going on," Cyrus said.

"Yeah, Boss, I hear you and I'm apologizing about that. I should have come to you," KC explained as Bruno let him go.

"How's your niece doing after the surgery?" Cyrus asked, taking the seat behind his desk.

"She's good, Boss. A guy my sister was seeing broke her arm and she was in the hospital a few days. I also had to pay off the social worker so that she wouldn't take my niece from my sister," KC admitted.

"What? You should have led with that in the beginning. Who is this guy? You know how I feel about things like that. Kids are always off limits."

Cyrus may not be living his life on the straight and narrow, but anything with harming kids was always dealt with swiftly.

"I know and I've been trying to take care of it," KC said.

"Well, you are a part of my team and she's a little girl. Give Bruno information on this guy and he'll take care of him. Go enjoy your night, get out on the streets and get my money and in a month, I expect to see every dime of it," Cyrus said.

"Thanks, Boss. I appreciate you, Boss."

"Bruno, go with him, get the information on this guy and let's see how he likes enduring some broken bones," Cyrus said.

When Bruno smiled, Cyrus knew it was because he enjoyed being the muscle and took delight in issuing pain.

"Got it, Boss," Bruno said, following KC out of the office. When the door opened, Kelly who works at the front door of the club stood on the other side.

"Kelly?" Cyrus addressed her.

"Boss, there is a woman at the door who asked me to give you this card. She said she's been trying to locate you and only knew how to reach you here at the club," Kelly explained.

Cyrus took the card from her hand and read it.

"Daniella Rice, Virginia Department of Child Services? She's looking for me?" he asked.

"Yeah. She asked if I would see if you were here and if she could speak to you for a few minutes. She didn't say exactly why, but I got the feeling it's personal, so I didn't ask. Do you want me to ask?" she asked.

“Is she alone?” he asked.

“She seems to be. No one was with her when she walked up to the window. You want me to tell her you’re not here?” Kelly asked.

“Nah. Jason, escort her up here. I don’t know what this is about, but if she came to D.C. and to the club this time of night, she’s really looking for me. If she has cops with her, text me. She only comes up if she’s alone,” he said.

Jason nodded and kept walking.

After everyone left, Cyrus read the name and organization from the card over and over again trying to wrack his brain to figure out why someone from Virginia with child services would be looking to speak with him. Walking over to the glass, he watched as Jason walked over to the front door of the club and a few seconds later, he emerged back on the path that led to the elevator that would bring them to the third level. Following behind him was a woman, looking like she was probably in the early to mid-forties. She was dressed in business attire, definitely not out for a night of partying. She even looked like she was ready to run away any second out of fear. Going back over to his desk, he sat down and waited.

“Child services?” he said out loud to himself. He wasn’t even sure he knew anyone in Virginia. Seconds later, the door to his office opened and in walked Jason followed by, who he assumed was the woman from the business card he still held in his hand.

"Mr. Cyrus Jackson?" she questioned, walking toward him, with her hand extended as she looked around nervously.

"Ms. Rice? I understand you're looking for me," Cyrus said, returning the hand shake and offering her a seat in one of the two leather chairs in front of his desk as he sat down behind his desk.

"Yes, and I'm sorry if I'm disturbing you here at your place of business. It's been a little hard finding you. I reached out to the Washington, D.C. Department of Child Services and they were taking too long to reach to you and so I took the drive here from Virginia. I shouldn't have because this isn't my jurisdiction, but it was necessary," she explained.

"Why are you looking for me? Your card said you're from Virginia child services? Are you sure you have the right person? The right Cyrus Jackson?" he asked.

"Let me explain. There was an accident a month ago in Richmond where a woman and her companion were killed. It was actually during a police chase, but that's a long story, one I don't want to get into tonight. Again, I'm not supposed to be here, but the livelihood of a little girl is on the line. That woman was the mother of this little girl. Does the name, Shiloh Johnson, ring any bells with you?" Daniella asked.

"No, it doesn't. Should it?" he asked.

"Well, according to information we have been able

to obtain, Shiloh's mother, Brenda Johnson, has listed you as Shiloh's father on her birth certificate, or someone name Cyrus Jackson, and one of her friends, who actually led us to you, said that she and Brenda were friends and that Brenda once confided in her that you were Shiloh's biological father. She even told us about this club that you own, which is how I found you," Daniella asserted.

Cyrus held his breath, not knowing how to respond to that. What he did know was that this was a private matter that didn't need an audience. He looked up at Jason.

"Jason, see if Kelly needs anything at the front and check on Oscar for me. If he arrives, tell him I'll be down in the basement shortly. Get him a bottle of something until I arrive. When you go out, make sure I'm not disturbed," Cyrus said to him, not taking his eyes from the woman in front of him.

"Got it," Jason said leaving without hesitation.

After the office door closed, Cyrus turned his full attention to his guest.

"Ms. Rice, I have no idea who Shiloh is or her mother, Brenda. You saying this to me is the first I'm hearing of it. Someone told you I was the father and that makes it so?" he asked.

"No, not at all. We can only go by what we are being told and I have to start someplace. It may or may not be you and if it's not, then I still have another Cyrus Jackson to look for, though your name isn't that common, at least not your first name. We have looked for over a month for any of Ms. Johnson's family and so far, we have come up empty. Apparently, Brenda left home at a young age and where that home is, we have no idea. There is no missing person's record and no one has come to claim her body," Daniella said.

"You said she was in some car chase?" he asked.

"She and her companion were running from the police after attempting to rob a local bank. She had left her daughter with a friend and that friend turned the little girl over to the police after hearing that Brenda died. I was able to get a little more information about this, if you'll bear with me. I need to look at my notes in my phone," she said.

"By all means, do. I need to be enlightened," Cyrus said leaning back in his chair. He didn't know if the woman was real and if her true purpose was about a child, but he was all ears. This could be some other kind of setup by way of law enforcement, but he would hear her out. He had a knack for scoping out shadiness and by the end of their conversation, he would know if she was being real or playing him. "How old is this little girl?" he asked.

"She's five-years-old. Her full name is Shiloh Antonia Johnson. She just turned five a few months ago and right now, she's a ward of the state of Virginia, living in a foster home. So, in my notes, after I spoke with her friend Jasmine a little more, she said that Brenda told her she met you one summer at a beach party in Virginia Beach. According to her, you hooked up a few times and Brenda got pregnant. There's a possibility that Brenda never told you about Shiloh. Jasmine recalls Ms. Johnson telling her that it wasn't anything serious with you and that after that weekend, she never saw you again, but she knew who you were and where you were, which is how we found you. She also listed you as the father on the birth certificate, though she had no other information on you other than your name. The police were able to find some papers after going through the house where Brenda and her companion lived. Those papers included Shiloh's birth certificate. After a more thorough search a week later, they found this picture of Brenda Johnson. It's an old picture, taken a few years ago," Daniella said, handing it to him.

Cyrus took the picture and then his past flooded back into his mind. He remembered Brenda and the night they took the picture while sitting on the sand in Virginia Beach. He remembered meeting her and spending an extremely wild and salacious weekend with her. That had been....

"Wow," he exclaimed.

"Is that you in the picture with Brenda?" Daniella asked.

"Yes, it is. I remember her now and you say this little girl is five?" he asked.

"Yes, she is."

"And you think she's mine?" he queried.

"I don't know, but if you will submit to a paternity test, we can end any doubt of whether she is or isn't," Daniella said.

Cyrus took a moment and soaked in the idea that as a result of a weekend of one sexual encounter after another with her, he'd fathered a child by her. Any doubt that he had over this woman sitting in front of him not being legit went out the window. His past was staring at him.

"And then what?" Cyrus asked.

"We're trying to find any family and then what's next is up to the courts to decide. Right now, she's a lonely little girl in the Virginia foster care system and let me tell you, from what I've heard and seen when it comes to her life, this little girl has lived the life of a grown person. She's seen too much and has been exposed to too much, so much in fact that she's terrified of everything and everybody. It's been over a month since her mother died and still, not once, has she asked for her mother. I've taken more of a personal stake in this case than I'm supposed to, but I've come to a point in my life where I want to fight for the rights of children and I want to make sure they have happy, productive lives with people they can call family. If that isn't you, then I apologize for wasting your time, but if she's your daughter, then my question to you would be, what will you do?" Daniella asked.

Cyrus leaned back in his chair and took in all he'd

just heard, looking at the picture once again, remembering how beautiful Brenda was and if he, in fact, had a daughter, he wanted to know more.

"Do you have a picture of Shiloh?" he asked.

"I can't give you a picture of her until after the paternity has been established and it turns out to be you. That's to protect her. I will say this, off the record, that now, after meeting you, she could be your twin from the light eyes to your overall face. It has been transplanted from you to that little girl. Until I saw you, I didn't know what to think. If you take the test and you're the father, you'll be able to see a picture of her and possibly see her without her seeing you, again to protect her. Anything after that is handled by the court in Virginia. Will you take a paternity test if I set it up for you?" Daniella asked.

A little girl that could be his? Someone walking around with his face? A little girl that could be his daughter and now in the foster care system? There was no doubt of what he would do.

"When?" he asked, looking over at Daniella.

"Monday morning," Daniella said.

Cyrus didn't know if Shiloh was his or not, but if Brenda had his baby and never told him about her, she was no longer around to explain to him why. His mind turned to KC and his niece who had been abused by a man who broke her arms; she was an innocent little girl. His first instinct was to hurt the man who had harmed her even though he didn't know her.

Now, he's being told he could possibly have a daughter that he never knew about who could possibly need him who was all alone in the world.

"Monday morning? You said she doesn't have anyone else?" he asked.

"No, she doesn't. She's in foster care with a woman who is one of our best foster parents, so she's fine, but that shouldn't be the life of any child if there is an alternative and a parent is an alternative and that could mean you. Will you help? If it's not you, at least I can then take another direction in finding other family. I'm starting with you because that's all I have to work with right now."

Cyrus looked at the picture again and looked at Brenda, who at that time was about twenty-three and he was twenty-seven at the time.

He remembered them talking about the four-year age difference, but he didn't care. He was hooked on her beauty the moment he saw her on the beach. She had long, black hair that flowed thickly around her shoulders. She had a big, beautiful smile and even then, she seemed lost, but fun. He remembered her telling him that she had been abused as a child and ran away from the west coast with another friend. He remembered the friend from that night but couldn't recall her name. He wondered what happened to her.

The night he'd met Brenda, there was a huge beach concert that he was attending with his crew from D.C. They had rented several beach houses on a private side of Virginia Beach. He'd seen Brenda and her friend dancing and swaying to the music and he couldn't take his eyes off of her. They spent the rest of the weekend in the house he had rented for himself. He'd rented other houses for those in his crew to share. He and Brenda spent all of their time in his house, in the bedroom, only venturing out for food. When he left on Sunday, he went back to his life in D.C. and he left her in Virginia with his number to call him to visit him in D.C., but she never contacted him. He now remembers giving her a business card from the club that he'd just purchased. She must have kept that and sometime later, shared that information with the friend who ended up with the little girl.

Looking over at Daniella Rice, he knew he had to know. How could he send his men out to knock a man down a peg or two for a little girl he didn't know and not find out if he had a daughter in the world who could possibly need him? He had to know.

"Yes. Monday morning is fine. Tell me where and I'll be there," Cyrus said and leaned back in his office chair. Monday already seemed like a million years away.

# 3 CHAPTER NAME

*Six Weeks Later*

Daniella walked up the long concrete walkway to the four red-brick steps that led to the gray painted concrete porch of Rose Moran's house while holding the folder in her hand that contained the results of the paternity test that Cyrus Jackson had been required to take if he wanted to know if he turned out to be the biological father of Shiloh. She'd spent weeks trying to find out as much as she could about Shiloh's mother and was sad to discover there wasn't much to find out.

There was no employment record for her, and it appears that when she gave birth to Shiloh, the only real records found on her, she had provided her name along with an address to an empty lot and a social security number that did not lead back to her, but to a number that had been made up. All they knew was that Brenda Johnson had arrived on the east coast from someplace on the west coast, but exactly where could not be determined. A check of records of anyone by that name being born around the time when she was born was taking a long time because of how common her name was. None of her friends knew anything about her life prior to showing up on the east coast, making her a true mystery. Even now, no one had shown up to claim Brenda's body. Daniella hated to think that Shiloh's mom would remain in a cold locker for ninety days while the state of Virginia waited for anyone to claim her body and if that didn't happen, she would be cremated and buried in a common grave with others who suffered the same fate. As she rang the doorbell and waited for Rose to answer, Daniella wished there as something she could do, but state law prevented her from getting that personally involved in any of her cases. Whatever happened to Brenda's body would be out of her hands.

"Daniella!" Rose exclaimed the moment the door opened.

"Hi, Ms. Rose. Is now still a good time to talk?" she asked.

"Yes, dear. Come on in. I just sat the kids down and they are all eating dinner. I was about to start a load of laundry. Come on into the sitting room. Can I get you something to drink? Water? Lemonade?" Rose asked.

"No, no. I'm fine," Daniella replied, entering a bright, sunny room to the right of the front door that had a wooden bench that went around the wall of the room from the entry on one side to the other side of the room. In the center was a small table with four chairs where she sat and placed her folder on the table after removing her coat.

"Give me a minute to check on the kids and I'll be right back," Rose said.

"You still have just three of them?" Daniella asked.

"Yes. Little Malcolm's grandmother was cleared and took over custody, so he's gone. I now have Shiloh, Charlotte and Destiny," she replied.

"I'm glad you had room for Shiloh. I needed someone patient like you for her," Daniella stated.

"I understand why. She's a sweet child and I'm sorry to hear she's lost her mother. I hope you have good news about her father. I'll be right back," Rose said and left the room.

Daniella opened manilla folder and flipped through the many documents, including the results of the paternity test. She wanted a minute to look through the medical report she received on Shiloh. With the exception of Shiloh being a little underweight and there being no record of the required shots, she was in great health. There were no traces of any kind of physical abuse, though records from the counselor found that Shiloh was afraid of everything and everyone. It was assumed that was a result of the life she led with her mother whose medical report was a totally different story.

Brenda, though her death was brutal, had traces of old wounds from two knife wounds that had not healed well and left large scarring on her leg and back. There were needle marks, signs of drug abuse which were fresh and some very old. Her body had been covered in old scars that were not a result of the accident. Her friend Jasmine had provided several pictures of Brenda and Daniella could tell that she was a very beautiful young woman who appeared to have lived a pretty rough life.

Her police record was also included and several of her arrests were under false names though they were able to link them together. Even her fingerprints didn't provide much by way of who she may be connected to before coming to Virginia. She was still a true mystery. The person who was not a mystery was Cyrus. His life was pretty much an open book. He also had prior convictions, but nothing within the past five years that was actually on record. He was on many radars due to what law enforcement believed were his ties to and involvement in illegal activities that included a major drug ring and money laundering. So far, no actual proof had been found, but assumptions were heavily on the record with the number of businesses he owned and ran with money that appeared to be untraceable. The Washington, D.C. area was prime for that type of activity.

"So, where were we?" Rose said, reentering the

room and sitting down.

Daniella smiled at the woman who reminded her so much of her own mother. Rose, like her mother always walked around with an apron on whether she was cooking or not. It was just a part of her look. She always had on house slippers and her hair was always pulled back into a neat bun. After raising her own son, Samuel, who had been killed overseas while serving in the military, she made it her life's mission to do what she could for other children, again filling her home with the laughter and love she once shared with her own son.

"We were about to talk about Shiloh and again, I want to thank you for taking her in. I know the hour was late and she arrived with pretty much nothing, but as usual, you saved the day. I'm sorry I was unable to bring much from her home, but everything was rodent infested," Daniella explained.

"Don't worry about it, child. I had plenty of things here for her and I already received money for her and we've gone shopping for some much-needed things for her and the rest of them. You know I'll never see these kids go without. My Samuel is smiling down on every child I bring across my door. He would have loved to have lived to see this," Rose said and exhaled loudly. Daniella gave her a minute while she reminisced about her son.

"I know your son is proud of the work you are doing with how you have opened your heart and your house to so many children," she said.

"I love each and every one of them and when it comes to this little one, this Shiloh, oh she is a doll. Still not talking much, but she listens well and is helpful. She doesn't sleep well and a few times I've found her asleep on the floor in the room next to the bed. I'm not sure what that's about, but I just put her back in bed whenever I find here there. I hear her mother died really tragic like. That's a shame. A little girl needs her momma. What about her father? Is it that young man you said you were going to contact?" Rose asked.

"Yes. I got everything here and there is no doubt he's Shiloh's biological father," Daniella said.

She smiled as Rose clapped and gave thanks as if she were in a church service.

"Oh, I'm so happy to hear that. What's next for him? Is he interested in being a part of this child's life? She needs more love in her life. I get the feeling she wasn't hugged much or really shown a lot of attention. She seems sad all the time like she's on guard. It's like someone prepared her to always be ready to go or run and hide or something. She's never just in the moment enjoying anything and every time a door opens, she practically jumps out of her skin. She must have had some kind of life," Rose said as she crossed her arms across her chest and rocked in her chair out of worry.

"We don't know the depths of it all, but in

conversations with a friend of Shiloh's mother, who has given us some insight, she said that Shiloh's mother rarely slept and pretty much lived in the streets, though she wasn't always that way. She said things turned bad for Brenda after meeting the man who was driving the car that killed them both. He introduced her to drugs and other criminal activity. She knew Brenda right after she gave birth to Shiloh and when she was still a little baby, that was when she met that man who was quite a few years older than her. He was in his forties, I think. Jasmine couldn't even count the number of places Brenda and Shiloh lived, never staying anywhere more than a few months and oftentimes, they squatted until they were kicked out, but in all of that, she always kept Shiloh with her and she always stayed in contact with Jasmine," Daniella explained.

"Do you think this fella would do right by her?" Rose asked.

Daniella had been thinking that same thought since she got the paternity test results along with the information that had been dug up on him. She always went with her gut and from the start of meeting him in the club that night when she told him about Shiloh, she didn't expect the response that she received and because she didn't, she had remained hopeful.

What she expected was for him to deny, deny, deny and then throw her out, but that's not what happened. He seemed genuinely concerned about

Shiloh and since the night she went to see him at his club, he'd reached out to her several times to ask how Shiloh was doing, even though he hadn't known if he was the father or not. The moment she called to let him know he was her father, he wanted to know what he could do to help her and whether or not he could see her. She informed him that he would have to wait for a notice to arrive for a court date and the judge would determine if he gets to see Shiloh that soon or if something else would have to be scheduled.

"He's kind of rough around the edges, but I have a feeling about him and it's a good one. I believe what I know about him on paper is not all there is to him. For the past month, he has checked in with me several times to ask how she's doing and when I told him that he was the father, he was ready to see her immediately, but I explained the process to him. I talked to him just yesterday when he called to say he received his notice for court which is in a week. Thankfully, my supervisor was able to get that date fast-tracked once paternity was established. He wanted to know if she'd been hurt or abused in any kind of way and if she needed anything. I feel like he really wants to do what's right. It's up to a judge to determine what that is. I think she'll look at his past and question what the right decision is. Whatever it is, it won't be an immediate one and he'll have to prove he's worthy. The bottom line, as usual, will be the best place for Shiloh to be. There is no family that we can find other than her father and it appears he really didn't know about her. I'm a true believer that he should be given a chance and Shiloh could use a win. She still hasn't asked about for her mother?" Daniella asked.

"She's barely said anything at all and no, she never mentions her. She does know that she died right?" Rose asked.

"Yes. She's been told and it's been explained to her that her mother dying means she'll never come back. So far, the doctor said there has been no reaction and no questions about her mother. She just seems to move on in her mind. I was hoping she would have asked something about her, but nothing, huh?"

Daniella had been worried since she heard that Shiloh had been told of her mother's death and yet, she hasn't longed for her mother at all. That's rare and odd, but then she had grown to expect the unexpected when it comes to children who end up being a part of her case load.

"Not one word. When will she be told that she has a daddy?" Rose inquired.

"Her doctor and her counselor will decide that and let me know. It will be sometime after the judge makes her initial ruling once the court has established on record that he's her father. I did tell Cyrus that once paternity was established, financially, he will be responsible for her and before I could get the full statement out of my mouth, he was telling me whatever the amount was, to double, triple or quadruple it, he didn't care. He only wanted to know if he could meet her. He said if there was anything she needed, to call him immediately. He understands that it could take quite a bit of time before anything leans in his favor and he understands that. Until then, he only wants to help where necessary. If you need anything for her, please let me know. I don't get many estranged parents who are willing to go above and beyond as he is, but then again, he's a new father and it's not like he walked away from her. I think he'll be good for her and more than that, I think she'll be good for him."

"You know I trust your judgement. It hasn't let us down yet and we've been working together a few years now and you've always been right in your assessment of parents. I want to see Shiloh smile. I haven't seen a smile since she arrived. She's pleasant and kind, but I don't think she knows how to just be a little girl and have fun. I'm hoping that finding her father will be the step in the right direction for them both," Rose said.

"When I finally located him, I went to see him at a club I was told he owned. When I was escorted to his office, I was questioning my recklessness of always acting instead of thinking things through. I was immediately intimidated just by his presence. He looked like the persona I assumed I would encounter and the people around him made him seem even more scary, but by the time I left, I felt like he wanted Shiloh to be his more than he wanted his next breath. After I spoke to him about the test proving she was his, I felt like this wasn't about finding family because Shiloh needed that, but the tables suddenly turned and I realized Cyrus needs Shiloh. I felt like he realized his life was missing something and Shiloh is the key. I'm pulling for them both," Daniella said and then turned back to the folder in front of her.

"I understand. You and I both know it's about the children and having a happy ending," Rose agreed.

"Yes, it is. Now, let's go over how Shiloh has been since I was last here two weeks ago and whether there is anything I should be concerned about. Also, I'll make sure you get the information on the court date as soon as I have it. If you like, I can come pick Shiloh up or if you want to take her, you can. I know you prefer to do that when you can," Daniella added.

"No worries. I'll bring her. I've enrolled her in school, but missing a day won't hurt much if it will get her closer to being with family. Let me get us some tea, I'll make sure the kids are done eating and can entertain themselves reading or something while we chat," Rose said standing.

"Tea sounds great."

Daniella knew even if she denied the request for something to drink a second time, Rose would bring it anyway. That's just how things went when she visited. She was also hoping to spend a few minutes with

Shiloh before she left. The conversation may end up being one-sided, but after already developing a soft spot for Shiloh, her welfare was a priority and secretly, she prayed that the little girl with the long black hair would smile one day. She had a feeling that smile would come when father and daughter could be united and given the time to find the love she felt they both needed.

# 4

## *Court Day*

Cyrus sat in the passenger seat of his customized, black Escalade truck outside of the Richmond, Virginia courthouse. He wasn't sure how he should feel about what was ahead of him. After confirmation was provided that he was in fact Shiloh's biological father, he went through emotions he'd never experienced before.

Before finding out about her, he didn't have any other children and wasn't sure he ever wanted any. His own disastrous childhood was a sign that he needed to avoid repeating for another child what he went through. His father was a hateful man who abused him and his mother and his mother took her aggression out on him after his father finally left him and his older brother, Marcus, with her to raise alone. Marcus, who was four years older than him had the kind of father he wished he'd had, but like his own father, Joseph Kane, their mother ran Kenneth Jackson, Marcus' father, away, not once, not twice, but three times after he came back again and again to try and make things work for the sake of his son. Though Kenneth was not his father, his mother gave him Kenneth's last name because at the time when she got pregnant by another man after she and Kenneth separated, her last name was still Jackson and so that ended up being his name.

While Marcus was able to escape being in their volatile house during times that he would stay with his father, Cyrus remembers being left to be in the middle of screaming matches, fist fights and dishes and mirrors being broken. He would get shoved around and whipped by his father and when his mother would get pissed at his father for hitting her or for seeing another woman, she would take over the whippings and beatings, just because. He happily left home during his junior year of high school, fleeing from North Carolina and following his brother Marcus to the D.C. area where Marcus was in college at Howard University. It was during that early time in D.C. that he found that life on the bad side of the law was what was going to sustain him in life. Since then, he'd prospered well in the drug game, enough that he had more money than he could ever spend and to be safe, he was cautious about where he spent it. Nothing about that life made him nervous or afraid to do what was needed to survive, but this taking on fatherhood was another story. He had no clue where to begin.

"Boss, are you going to sit here in the truck or go inside? I need to find a place to park before a cop walks up and makes me move the truck. You nervous or something?" Jason asked.

Cyrus turned toward him and tossed the middle finger his way, sending them both into a fit of laughter. Jason had been his boy since the first day he arrived in D.C. After begging Marcus to take him in and then finding living with his studious brother wasn't going to work, he had befriended Jason who let him camp out at the house where he lived with his mother in a rough part of D.C.

Jason was small in stature at five-foot-five and was often picked on. Cyrus, who was already six-feet-tall at sixteen, would beat guys down who picked on the sixteen-year-old and from day one, they became best friends. Jason was the one person he trusted, not just with his secrets, but with his life. They had come up in the game together and if anyone had his back in everything in life, it was Jason. He wished he could say the same for his brother and his mother, both he hadn't spoken to in a few years.

"So, the answer is you're going to sit here?" Jason inquired again.

"Fool, I'm getting out. We're early, so I have time. Court isn't until ten and it's just nine. I'm just wondering if coming here was a good choice. What am

I going to do with a kid, man? You know my life and not only that, but she's a girl," Cyrus questioned.

"You could have said no, paid the child support they are going to get from you anyway because she's in the system and kept it moving. Let her go to a good family, if that's what you want to do. On the other hand, she's yours, dude. I know you didn't know about her, but do you seriously want to let someone else raise her knowing she's yours? You said this social services lady told you they believe your daughter had a horrible upbringing with that Brenda chick. Did she go into detail?" Jason asked.

"After she called to say the paternity test came back that I was the father, she shared a little about Shiloh and I forgot to show you the picture they sent me."

Cyrus reached into the glove compartment and pulled out the folder with the picture and other small details about his daughter. He handed the picture to Jason and opened the folder.

"Damn, bro. She is literally your twin! What the hell was that chick Brenda thinking not telling you about her? She had to see you every time she looked in her daughter's face."

Cyrus thought the exact same thing the minute he received the picture. He was told the picture had been taken sometime in the last two weeks. To say Shiloh looked like him was an understatement. When he looked at the picture, except for the long, thick, black hair, he was looking into his own face. More than that, his daughter could also pass as a twin to his niece, Mariah, who should be seven now. He hadn't seen her in two years when she was five, the same age Shiloh is now. There was no doubt that Shiloh was his flesh and blood.

"She also looks exactly like my niece, Mariah. You know, I tossed most of the night and ended up sleeping in my office at the club. I went in to go over the books and handle some calls and I found myself unable to concentrate. I could only think about Shiloh being in some group home or in some foster home with a bunch of people she didn't know. She must be scared."

"Did her rough life include any kind of abuse or anything?" Jason asked.

Cyrus shook his head no, vigorously. He was happy to hear that no one had laid a finger on his daughter or he would be out for blood. He tried to tamper down his murderous rage because he has a daughter to think about now and he was glad he didn't have to tap into that part of himself.

"None. According to her case worker, she's small for her size as far as her weight, but that's pretty much it. They don't think she was getting fed on a consistent basis. Her medical checkup came back okay, but she's been seeing a child psychiatrist who still has not gotten a word out of her. She also sees a counselor. They know that she can talk, but she's very shy and afraid of some adults. She only seems to warm up to her case worker, Ms. Rice."

"What else do you know about her?" Jason asked handing him the picture back.

Cyrus didn't immediately put it away, but held it in his hand and looked into the unsmiling, frightened face of his daughter. He was still trying to get familiar with the idea that he had a kid.

Cyrus flipped through more pages that had been emailed to him about Shiloh.

"Her full name is Shiloh Antonia Johnson. Her birthday was in August, on the second. She was in daycare for pre-kindergarten last year, but according to the records, she missed more than half of the days. She doesn't talk much, so they don't know a whole lot about what she knows and doesn't know. They ask her questions about numbers, colors, letters, stuff like that and she can point out the correct answers, but she won't actually say anything. So far, she hasn't related much to the other kids where she's living in Richmond. Her case worker visits with her once a week and they seem to have bonded. They also note that she loves to eat chicken nuggets and French fries. She also loves bananas. As of right now, they still haven't been able to find any of Brenda's family and they doubt that they will. She's been estranged from her family since her teen years and there has never been any record of anyone looking for her. I remember when I met Brenda, she told me that she hated her life before Virginia and didn't want to talk about any family or friends from before. Shiloh is alone in the world," Cyrus lamented.

Every time he looked at her picture, his heart ached for the loneliness he saw in her eyes; eyes that looked like his own. He's had times in his life where he felt alone and lonely and most were when he was a kid living at home with his mother. She was unloving and uncaring unless it came to Marcus. For him, she never had enough love to go around. He could imagine that the sadness he saw in Shiloh's face in her picture was what he would have looked like if someone had taken his picture back then.

Like her, he knew what it felt like to be alone. The difference was, he had family out in the world, but with the issues he's had with them over the years, he preferred to stay away. One thing was for sure and that was his brother, Marcus, his wife, Shamari and their two kids, Mariah and Carmelo would love Shiloh. She would no longer have to be alone in the world. He made the decision to show up in court today to make sure she never felt alone again.

Slipping the picture of Shiloh into the jacket pocket of the black velour sweat suit he wore, Cyrus reached for the door handle to get out.

"I'll park and find you. You think they'll give you your kid today?" Jason asked.

"Man, I don't know what to expect. I was told to be here and I'm here," Cyrus responded.

Standing outside of the car, Cyrus reached down and used a napkin from the box on the dashboard to wipe off a small smudge on his new white Jordan's. The platinum chain with the large head of a lion on it around his neck dangled and gleamed in the bright sun of the chilly October day.

"You look like you can take care of her. You have on more bling than Diddy wears!" Jason joked.

Cyrus looked at the rings on his fingers with diamonds glistening, to the platinum bracelets on his wrist and the chain around his neck. He couldn't see the diamonds in his ears, but he knew they were there. He was being him and if the courts decided against him, it wouldn't be because he couldn't financially take care of Shiloh. His guilt was around not being able to take care of her because he didn't know how. Would he even make a good father?

"Whatever. I'll see you inside. The room we're in is on the fourth floor. Don't come in late."

"Cy – can I ask you a question without it pissing you off?" Jason asked.

"What?"

"Do you think you should have called your brother? I mean, Marcus is a lawyer and everything and he could probably help," Jason asked.

Cyrus exhaled and looked in all directions around the car. He hadn't thought about checking with his brother. He had given up on connecting with his family years ago when they constantly put him down because of the illegal lifestyle he lived. He was tired of explaining himself and feeling like he owed his family anything. Chats with his mother were hit and miss over the years. With his brother, they had gone through lots of ups and downs and though Marcus meant well, Cyrus didn't like feeling like a failure whenever he was around his successful lawyer of a brother.

"I haven't talked to my brother in two years. I've talked to his wife who has been trying to broker a reconnection between us, but that's been over a year and a half, but you know how crazy life has been and Marcus is too judgmental. I can't handle that right now. I'm not pristine clean in my life like he and his family with their house in the suburbs and kids in private school. I don't want to hear him talking about how I couldn't know that I had a kid out in the world."

"He's family, bro, that's all I'm saying. I'll be up in a minute," Jason said.

Cyrus closed the car door and turned toward the building he was buying time to enter. It was now or not now, he thought as he walked toward the door to where another room full of people will judge him. He wasn't sure he was ready for it, but Shiloh was his daughter and he wanted to see her. His only chance at doing that was to go through the process. Even if they decided against him taking care of her from this point on, he hoped he would have a chance to see her in person and not just by way of the photo in his pocket.

**

Daniella sat on a bench outside of the courtroom with Shiloh's court appointed attorney, Shana Maddox, who will represent Shiloh's interest.

"What should I expect today? I know this isn't new for me, but this little girl literally has no one other than me and Ms. Rose and now that we know who her father is, I'm hoping he's more than the background we've turned up on him," Daniella said as she shifted nervously in a suit with a skirt that was a little too tight for sitting and a jacket that was a little snug on her arms.

"Daniella, you need to exhale. I know how you get with your clients and I can tell this little girl has already worked her way into your heart and you want her out of foster care," Shana exclaimed.

Daniella slumped back on the bench and tried to gather herself. She, too, could feel herself getting worked up.

"I want every child out of foster care and into homes where they can be loved and adored and Shiloh deserves that plus more. She's been through a lot for a five-year-old and we have been unable to find any family on her mother's side, so this guy is it. I looked at the background on him and he's literally feared on the streets of D.C. We've tried talking to people and they either have glowing things to say about him as if it's scripted and he's some sort of god or they run from us scared and holding up their hands like they surrender and would rather go to jail than answer any questions. The investigator said on many occasions he's had to prove that he's not the police when talking to people, but still, people say things like they care too much about their family's lives and their own lives to risk it by saying anything about him. The investigator called him notorious. If anyone mentions Cyrus' name on the streets, there isn't a person who doesn't know who he is or a person who doesn't fear for their life if they say anything against him. Is that the right environment for a little girl, even if it's her father? What her mother's life was like and what Shiloh may have been exposed to in the past five years is enough. Do you know that they've tried bringing charges against him several times in the past and nothing has stuck in over five years? There are claims that he has cops on the take who protect him and warn him of what's coming his way. He's now covering his ill-gotten way of life with legit businesses, but still, what they claim he has done and is responsible for is dangerous. What could that mean for Shiloh if the judge turns her over to him?" Daniella asked, speaking so fast she was practically out of breath and she was sitting down.

She felt a reassuring tug on her arm from Shana.

"Breathe, Daniella. It's going to be okay. This guy can't live that life and expect the court to turn a five-year-old little girl over to him. The choice will be left up to him to decide what's worth more to him, that life or being a father to a little girl who has no one else, and I mean no one else."

Daniella followed Shana's eyes and saw that they had landed on Cyrus as he walked the hallway toward the courtroom doors which were still closed. He recognized her and gave her a nod. Seeing him in his street hustler attire wasn't what she was expecting. Following him was another man, much shorter, one she remembered from the night she went to the club to talk to Cyrus. Both, clearly, had no clue of what they were about to be confronted with in a courtroom.

"Yeah, he's a sinking ship. Look at how he's dressed and all that bling? For what? To show he has money?" Daniella questioned.

"Like I said, calm down and pull it back. You're too in your feelings and this is not a Drake video production. This guy will get a lesson real fast, but trust me, he'll have time to get it together. This isn't an overnight process and if he really wants his daughter, he's going to have to prove it and work for it. I'm going to see to that and I have no doubt the judge will too. The doors are opening. Let's head inside and try not to react on feelings. This is not your first rodeo and you know what, Shiloh could be dealing with a worse parent. Yeah, he's a pretty rough character and I can tell that he uses his appearance and presence to demand respect, but he'll find today that just like other courtrooms where he's been the defendant, no one will care about his street status.

Here, justice rules and he'll either play right and do the right thing or he'll see his daughter placed with a family who deserves a beautiful little girl like her," Shana said.

Daniella nodded, stood and straightened her skirt and her face and followed Shana into the courtroom, keeping her eyes glued on Cyrus as she took a seat in the back of the room until the judge called her name.

# 5

Cyrus stood as the judge continued to flip through page after page in front of her as she sat behind her desk holding the fate of him and his daughter in her hands. The moment her eyes set on him, he saw her judgment. He also knew that they had been digging into his life and knew that the judge wasn't going to like what was discovered about his life. His time in jail back in his teen years was not a public record, but he was sure she'd gotten her hands on it anyway and he knew that his other skirmishes with the law were also on record, including short stints in prison in his early twenties. Was he fit to even take care of anyone other than himself? He wasn't sure, but he didn't want to be judged by anyone else. He was doing enough judging of his own life after finding out he had a daughter and he could possibly lose her to the same system that prosecuted him over the years.

"Mr. Jackson."

Cyrus stood up straight, cleared his throat and held his head of high.

“Yes, ma’am,” he replied after hearing his named called.

“I see that you recently were told that your daughter existed and so far, you are the only family the state of Virginia has been able to locate. I understand you’re petitioning to secure parental rights and at the applicable time, retain custody of the minor child known as Shiloh Antonia Johnson. Is that correct?” the judge asked.

“Yes, Judge Mathers,” Cyrus said, glad with himself that he caught her name when it was stated at the start of the case. He’d already been in the room for over an hour as the case was read out loud from the start of what they knew about the car crash and moving forward from that day. He listened to the report from the child psychiatrist who talked about her sessions with Shiloh and how they were going. He heard the written report that was read on behalf of Shiloh’s foster mother who noted that though Shiloh was no trouble, she preferred time alone in a corner away from everyone else. He paid attention as Daniella Rice went over the notes in her file of what was discovered about his life and he cringed as the words were read out loud of all the infractions he had been accused of and some that he’d been convicted of. He didn’t think this was the place to air all of that, but he held his composure. Thankfully, nothing was new within the past few years since he learned how to hide his dirty business from prying eyes of public officials. He wasn't squeaky clean by any means, but him being a hardened criminal was only on paper.

"I see here that you have had some run-ins with the law since you were sixteen years old. Though I see nothing new, there are some questions about how you make your money," she stated.

"Yes, well I own several reputable businesses," he interjected.

"I see that, but the issue here from the investigation was how you acquired the funds to get these businesses up and running. There are no records of business loans or anything close to that. Can you explain how you got the funds to start these businesses? You're thirty-two and doing well for yourself, but I'm concerned about how you got here. I see you file taxes, but before all of this, where the money came from is my questions," Judge Mathers stated.

Cyrus was losing patience. Why was his life on display? This was supposed to be about Shiloh. Why did anyone care how he made his money? He had more than enough to care for Shiloh, though most of what he had, there was no way they would have a record of that, but the amounts they did know about were more than sufficient to make a case for financial responsibility for his daughter. They would only have found financial records of legal transactions and not the funds he made sure there was no record of. Shouldn't the only thing that mattered at this point is if he could take care of his daughter?

"I don't understand why that matters," he said, showing his lack of patience with the process.

"Mr. Jackson, it matters to this court. This little girl has been through enough trauma in her life to last a lifetime and I would have a problem putting her in a situation where things aren't quite on the up and up. I understand that you own two-night clubs that are open until two in the morning. Is that correct?" she asked.

"Yes, that's correct and both turn a great profit. I live a good life and so would my daughter," he explained.

"That may be true. Do you personally oversee these nightclubs each night?" she asked.

"Yes, I do."

"Okay. Now, we're getting somewhere. So, if you're at these clubs from, what eight or nine at night until two or three in the morning and you had your daughter with you, who is looking after her during those hours? I don't see any family with you here today and though I understand you do have family, you have been hesitant about providing information for them to be contacted and interviewed. I also see that you don't have any other children. Is that correct?" she asked.

Cyrus exhaled loudly and looked down at the table

he stood behind. He quickly looked around behind him and saw Jason sitting in the back row, but other than him, the psychiatrist, the case worker, the bailiff and the judge, no one else was in the court and not a single person to support him. The question Jason asked about his family rang loud in his head. He had no one – just as Shiloh didn't.

"That's correct. As far as I know, I don't have any other children," he answered.

"And your family?" she asked.

"We're estranged at the moment," he quickly replied.

Cyrus tried to not let his immediate hatred for the judge show on his face, but he had a feeling he was losing that struggle. From the way she was glaring at him over her thick rimmed glasses, she was letting him know that she was ready to tell him that turning Shiloh over to him would be the last thing she would do. He saw her hatred for him and what she already knew he did to make money, but didn't say. His lifestyle was all over the papers in her file, but like law enforcement, there was no real proof because he was smooth like that.

"No family, no friends to help with this little girl. I assume the man at the back of the room is with you. You seem to be dressed alike today. Is he not family?" she asked.

Cyrus felt the disdain in her words, but let it go.

"He's a loyal friend," Cyrus replied, looking from

Jason, to Daniella Rice, who refused to look his way. He then looked back at the judge.

"Loyal friends don't count. One of the issues I have is that this little girl came from an environment where she didn't have any family other than her mother and the man who was driving the car that crashed and killed them both. Now, here you are, in my courtroom coming as the only person she would again have in the world and that's not enough. Knowing what I believe I know about your lifestyle, I would hate for this little girl to again end up without a parent because of *that* life that you appear to be proud of. This little girl needs more in her life. She needs much, much more. You would have to sacrifice a lot which means being at home at night, all night with her. Spending less time running your businesses and you do have quite a few of those that probably take up a lot of your time. Though I can tell by the way you're dressed today with enough diamonds and bling to blind me from behind my bench, raising a child is not about money. It's about more than that. Do you know what some of those other things are?" she asked.

Cyrus knew he didn't have a clue. He didn't have a childhood to use as an example.

"Maybe, I don't, but she's my daughter. You all came looking for me. I didn't come looking for this and I'm here. I showed up today," he responded.

"Oh, did you have someplace else to be that's more important or as important as what's going on here today with your daughter? Some big business deal or other type of transaction that this court should know about and feel sympathy for you over that you had to make a sacrifice and be here today? Yes, Mr. Jackson, you showed up today and that's the easy part. The hard part is what would you do with Shiloh if you were given custody of her? She has to go to school, something her mother didn't do a good job of making sure happened on a consistent basis. She needs to know and feel loved. She needs to see the good part of life. She needs stability. She needs a parent who will be there, not another parent who will leave her with others to go about their life. She's been through that. There's so much more she will need outside of doctor appointments, weekly appointments with a counselor, a psychiatrist and possibly a tutor for school. Kids need a lot more than just money and bling, though, again from your appearance, I can see that you have plenty of both. Neither will give a child the comfort of knowing she won't be bounced around again. I understand you live in a condo of which I'm told is a real party scene some nights. Will your daughter be living in that atmosphere? Do you get that I expect more than what I've already learned about you? This court is not impressed. *I* am *not* impressed, Mr. Jackson" the judge said.

Cyrus was even madder now as he balled his fist up and then relaxed them when the judge looked down to where his hands were. He had to be careful about showing aggression which was his go-to response to anyone who questioned him.

"Judge, no disrespect, but people have kids every day and don't go through this. Where was the court when her mother wasn't doing right by her?" he asked.

"Where were you?" the judge retorted loudly.

"I didn't know about her!" Cyrus shouted before realizing how loud he was being.

"Exactly and we didn't know about her either, but that doesn't mean that now that we know about her that we won't make sure that she is placed in the hands of someone who will now do right by her. I don't know if that's you. You show up looking like a rapper laced in enough jewelry to feed a small nation. Your attire today is a statement that you have money and that you feel that money will get you what you want no matter how you appear. You don't show up with any kind of representation though it was suggested that you seek counsel to make sure you understand what these proceedings would be like. I see that you're angry over my questions and how I'm approaching you and this isn't about you, it's about your daughter. You come here today without any kind of support other than a loyal friend and that's not enough. You have family that you're estranged from, but this isn't a time for pride. You should have reached out to them and if you're going to really take care of your daughter, you are going to need that; you are going to need family. This court will need to see that. I can't make your family whole, but having family as support will go a long way with this court. What I'm going to do today is issue a postponement of this court's decision in the matter of Shiloh Johnson. I will allow you to visit with her starting today. You can have one day a week, two hours each week of supervised visits with her. I would prefer that these visits take place at her counselor's office where her interactions with you can be monitored. You will have four weeks of two-hour visits and we'll reconvene in this courtroom in thirty days to hear about these visits. For now, the minor will remain with her foster mother who will make sure she is on time for your weekly visits. If you miss even one of your visits, I will issue another thirty-day postponement for each visit you miss. If you miss more than three, the court will render its decision based on your lack of availability to your daughter. Do you have a day of the week that you're not too busy to make the trip from D.C. to Richmond? I wouldn't want to impede on your ability to run any of your many business ventures," the judge said snidely.

Cyrus felt that stab of her words, but held his head up. He'd had enough of the world thinking he was incapable of caring and doing the right thing. He didn't know Shiloh, but he was already thankful for her. If he needed to make sacrifices for her, he would do it not because he was being told to, but because he wanted to do the right thing. Brenda may not have done right, but he would prove that Shiloh had a parent who was willing to sacrifice everything just for her. He may not know how to do it, but he was open to learning and that starts today.

"Pick any day and any time and I'm there. I will not miss even one of those appointments and I'll be on time, if not early for every single one of my visits. Do I get to see her today? I don't want to overwhelm her and I'm okay if you don't want her to see me yet, but can I at least set my eyes on her. I know you don't have much faith in me and that's understandable. You and I both know what my life is like without having to say it, but this little girl needs someone and today and every day after today, she'll have me even if you don't render in my favor. I'm still her father and I will make sure that I will be a presence in her life no matter what you decide. I believe I am entitled to that as her father. I'm willing to do whatever it takes. I showed up here not knowing what to expect or what I should have done and that's on me, but that won't happen again," Cyrus expressed.

"Well, well, I see you have your second wind. That all sounds good. I like your spunk and determination. I wasn't expecting that, but it's good to see you're really taking this seriously. I look forward to seeing you come through. I'm also going to require parenting classes for you. She's not an infant – she's five years old. You need to know what to expect. Ms. Rice can refer you to places to take the required classes and you'll also be required to sit down with a counselor once a week for an hour. You can ask for a referral or you can find one on your own. I'll expect that report in thirty days. You will be able to see and talk to Shiloh today if you like. She's here at the courthouse in one of our playrooms. You'll have an hour to visit with her, but be warned that you should not pressure her into liking you or talking to you or anything close to that. You have to go at her pace. There is an outer room where you can see her without her seeing you and if that's enough for you for today, do that. You can also go into the room and sit with her and talk to her, but keep it light talking about fun things like toys or foods she likes to eat. You will have plenty of time to talk to her about being her father. She has not been told about that yet, but she will be told when her doctor thinks it's the right time. Is that clear, Mr. Jackson?" she asked.

Cyrus wanted to smile because he was finally getting the chance to see Shiloh. Inside, his mind was doing a happy dance. There was this new side of him that even he didn't recognize. He was tapping into a part of him where he didn't know feelings existed, but here he was, standing in a courtroom pleading for a chance to prove himself. He was feeling love for a person other than himself. He had a daughter who needed him and even though his history didn't dictate that he was unselfish, he was all set to make Shiloh his one and only priority. He didn't know where the idea came from, but the moment he got word that Shiloh was his daughter, the hardened heart he'd been walking around with broke open and out poured the love for someone else other than himself.

"Crystal clear, Judge and I apologize for my aggression. Thank you," he said.

"Good. I'm glad you showed up today, Mr. Jackson, but a word of caution – seek representation before you show up again and next time, leave the bling at home. I know you have it, but it means nothing when it comes to the love that child needs.

"Yes ma'am," Cyrus said.

"We're adjourned," the judge said and Cyrus turned to Daniella who walked over to him.

"Would you like to see Shiloh now?" she asked him.

"Yes, I would." He turned to Jason. "I'll meet you outside in a few ticks," he said and then followed Daniella out of a side door.

"Shiloh is in a playroom, as the judge stated. Each time we have court, she will be brought here. For your weekly session with her, I'd like to establish that day and time before you leave so that it coincides with her weekly counseling sessions. There is a nice room that makes children feel comfortable where you can meet with her. As the judge stated, please don't miss a session or be late for one. Judge Mathers does not play and she hates excuses. Shiloh deserves dedication and stability and if you can't give that, then don't get her hopes up after she finds out you're her father. She's had enough let downs in life. Okay, here is a pass to get into the area where Shiloh is. I actually got this ahead of time hoping the judge would let you see her. I know you've been wanting to see her for some time now and I wanted to make that happen for you. You'll have an hour. I suggest you take a moment and observe her from the viewing room before going in. I will warn you that Shiloh is extremely shy and she still doesn't know how to play along with other children yet. She loves dolls and she loves books. She also loves to color. Feel free to read to her or color with her. She'll like that. When I have my visits with her, we always color and she lights up when I bring her new coloring books. If you have any questions, I'll be there shortly. I have some paperwork to file and get copies of. Her foster mother is Ms. Rose and she'll be in the viewing room if you want to meet her. You cannot ask her questions about where she lives or anything else personal. Focus on Shiloh, okay?" Daniella asked.

"Whew! There are a lot of rules, but I understand why. I just want to see her. It's been a rough month of not knowing and now that I'm here, I didn't think I would be ready, but I am. I want to see her," Cyrus said.

"Great. Go through the double doors to your left, show your pass and identification and you'll be escorted to the viewing room. Good luck, Mr. Jackson.

Shiloh is a beautiful little girl and I'm glad she's your daughter," Daniella said turning and walking away.

When she was out of ear range, Cyrus smiled.

"So am I," he muttered and turned toward the double doors.

# 6

Rose looked up as the door to the viewing room opened and in walked the man she now knew was Shiloh's father. She smiled and greeted him as he smiled at her once he closed the door behind him.

"I'm Rose Moran. It's nice to meet you, Mr. Jackson."

Cyrus extended his hand to shake the hand she extended out to him.

"Please call me Cyrus. Thank you for looking after Shiloh."

"You want me to point her out to you?" Rose asked from the chair in the far corner of the lighted room, a distance from the glass window that separated the two rooms, the one they were in and the one Shiloh was in.

"No, I know what she looks like from the picture I was given," he said walking over to the window.

"She looks just like you. The resemblance is

uncanny. Looking at you is like looking at her without the long hair," Rose quipped.

"I know," Cyrus said looking around the room for Shiloh.

He counted six children up and running around the room, playing together and none were Shiloh. To the far right, he saw her, sitting in a corner between two corner book cases. She wasn't playing or reading. She was sitting alone in the corner with her legs tucked under her looking down at the floor. Her hair was in two long, thick braids. She had on a black t-shirt and blue denim jeans that looked like they were a size too big. Her hands were playing around with the shoe strings of her sneakers. She looked alone and Cyrus felt his heart clinch as if it were in pain. He felt her sorrow through the thick pane of the glass. His heartbeat sped up and he anxiously wanted to give her a hug and tell her that he was her father and he was here for her. He wondered what happened in her life that had her distancing herself from everyone even other children.

"She's still sitting in that corner?" Rose asked.

"Yes. Is she always like that?" Cyrus asked standing so close to the glass that his breath caused steam to form on it.

"Yes, she is. I have three other kids at the house. They're older than her, but still, she doesn't like to interact with them. She prefers to sit still as if she's always being punished for something. Her counselor mentioned to me that it's possible she was told to sit like that by herself all the time. She also has this thing about sleeping on the floor. I put her in bed, but then in the morning, I'll find her asleep on the floor in the corner. My heart goes out to her. She's a hearty eater though. She's a beautiful child, very sweet. She never gives me any kind of problem."

"She looks lonely; she looks alone," Cyrus uttered quietly as his own heart began to bleed for the little girl with the sad looking eyes. He knew immediately that one of the biggest jobs before him was to change that. He had to figure out how to bring light to her eyes.

"She's not alone any more. She has you now. I don't know you, but you've done something that not many have done or will do – you showed up," Rose said.

"Should I go in? I don't want to scare her?" he asked.

"Yes, go in and even if you just sit with her and talk to her about toys or cartoons or pick up a book and read it, she'll love that. She may not have a reaction and she probably won't talk to you or even look at you, but she needs someone to be present. Sometimes when I'm cooking and the other kids are running around playing, she'll come into the kitchen and sit at the table and watch me. She doesn't want to talk or play – she just wants to be there. Even though she doesn't respond, I still hold an entire conversation with her, going through what I'm cooking and how I'm cooking it. I sometimes talk about a show I watched on television, usually some cartoon or another that she would enjoy hearing about. I also play music and when she thinks I'm not listening, I'll see her little body swaying to the music. If I look at her, she won't move."

"I love television and music. I own a music production studio and oversee making all kinds of music," he said.

"She loves music too. Sometimes she hums tunes, mostly Beyonce and I think she's an old soul because she loves music by Luther Vandross and the Temptations," Rose laughed.

"Wow! That's crazy! Those are two of my favorite artists of all time. I listen to Luther and the Temptations all the time," Cyrus smiled.

He loved that he already had something in common with his daughter. They already had a crazy connection.

"Go ahead in. I can see it in your body language that you're dying to get in there. You only have an hour, so don't waste it standing here talking to me," Rose exclaimed.

Cyrus grinned so wide, his cheeks had a quick, sharp pain in them. He wasn't sure he'd ever smiled that bright before. Turning around, he went through a single door that led to another single door that led to the inside of the playroom. The aide in the room looked in his direction and he pointed to Shiloh and showed her his badge that had Shiloh's name on it. When the aide nodded her head and went to the other side of the room, he walked to a small table that sat in front of the corner where Shiloh sat. He looked around at the room full of books, toys and stuff animals. He didn't know what to do, but he needed something to ease him into Shiloh's space. Seeing a pink, plush elephant, he picked it up and walked toward her. Instead of standing and crowding her with his height, he sat cross-legged in front of her on the floor. She didn't look at him, which he expected, but he persevered. Since she didn't know who he was, he assumed she would think he was another counselor.

"Hello, Shiloh. My name is Cyrus and I hope it's okay that I'm sitting here with you. I'm so tall that these little chairs would break if I sat on one. I have a friend here with me. He doesn't have a name or anything, but I thought he was cute and you might like him. Do you want to see him?" he asked.

Cyrus waited but got no response, as he expected.

"Okay, well, I'll hold him for now. Your hair is pretty. I bet it would look really pretty with some ribbon or flowers in it. I've seen little girls with those things in their hair and they like them. I like pink and white or maybe yellow. Do you like ribbons or flowers in your hair?" he asked.

Still no answer.

"Maybe pink like this elephant? I was told you also like to color. When I was a little boy, I loved to color. I went to a school and we would use crayons all day. That was one of my favorite things to do. I think I'll find a book and some crayons and do a little coloring? Maybe you can color with me? If not, it's okay."

Cyrus reached to the left of him and picked up a couple of coloring books from the bottom shelf of the three-shelf bookcase. There was a pencil case full of crayons already on the table. He picked it up and sat the case between them on the floor. Taking one of the books, he placed one in front of her and one in front of him. He opened the book and opened the pencil case.

"I think I'll start with red. This book has a picture of Bert and Ernie from Sesame Street in it and one of them is red. I'm not sure which one is supposed to be red. Can you help me with that? Do you know which guy is red and which one is yellow?" Cyrus asked, holding the book up between them with the page facing her. He wasn't expecting an answer, but he would keep talking to her like Daniella suggested he do.

He was about to put the book back down on the floor to start coloring when he saw her hand moving. Without looking up at him, Shiloh pointed to the page at Ernie and to Cyrus, his entire world just expanded. He wanted to jump up and do a dance because Shiloh responded to him after everyone said she doesn't respond to anyone.

"That's him?" he laughed. "I'm glad you helped me, Shiloh, because I would have colored Ernie yellow and he wouldn't like that. So, besides coloring, which I'm told you like to do, I hear you like books and dolls. Do you have a favorite?" Cyrus asked as he began coloring. He stretched to ease the pain of sitting with his legs crossed and leaning over to color.

"I like books and music. Maybe one day you can pick out a book for me to read to you – something you like? Maybe, a story about a princess. Little girls like princesses and I bet you do too. I like all kinds of books, not really those about princesses, but I would enjoy reading one to you. The coloring book in front of you has a lot of princesses in it, if you want to color one. You can pick any color you want from the box. What do you think? I like this Bert and Ernie book, but I think I'm messing up this coloring thing. I keep going outside of the lines," he laughed and smiled when for a brief second, Shiloh looked over at him and then looked back down at the floor.

As he continued coloring and talking, the tried to talk about everything from food to books to dolls as time dwindled down to where he was going to have to leave. He may not have made any headway with her, but at least he got to see her in person and even had the chance to talk to her. He pulled from his days of playing with his niece before he stopped going around them and remembered the things that Mariah liked to talk about. When he finished coloring, he held the book up so that Shiloh could see it just in case she looked up from the place on the floor that garnered her attention.

"Well, looks like I'm finished this one of Ernie. I guess I need to find a yellow crayon to color in Bert so that he's not the only one with no color. I wonder what yellow I should use? Could you help me pick one?" Cyrus asked.

He waited without moving and continued to hold the book up. Just before he lowered it, he again saw Shiloh move a little. His heart swelled with love when she reached into the pencil box and pulled out a yellow crayon and handed it to him. He turned and looked toward the glass window to the room where Ms. Rose was and wondered if she was watching them and was as happy as he was that Shiloh was reacting to him. He had a feeling she was watching and just as happy as he was. Turning back to Shiloh, he was even more shocked to see that she had opened up the coloring book in front of her, picked a pink crayon from the box and began coloring a princess on the first page.

"Ah, you do love pink, huh. I like that color too. I only have a few more minutes to sit here with you, but when I have to leave, I hope it's okay that I come visit you again. I like coloring with you. Ms. Rose said I can come visit again and I look forward to doing that. Maybe the next time, I can bring you some of those pink ribbons or pink flowers to put in your hair that that princess had in the picture you're coloring. Would you like that?" he asked.

Shiloh nodded her head yes and continued to color.

Cyrus' mind did a happy dance.

"I'll find some that are very pretty just like you. I think I'll color one more picture before I go."

For a few minutes, Cyrus stopped talking and just colored. He watched her color a full picture and when they were finished, he tore his picture from the book and laid it in front of her.

"I'm going to leave you my picture because you have been so nice to me by coloring with me. This is a present from me to you. I hope you like it, Shiloh," he said. "I have to leave because Ms. Rose needs to get you back to her house so that you can get something to eat. Remember my name is Cyrus and I'll see you again soon. It was nice to meet you, Shiloh," he said standing.

Cyrus turned around and placed the coloring book back on the shelf. When he turned back around to face Shiloh, she sat with her arm stretched out to him, holding the picture that she'd colored and torn from the coloring book out to him.

"This is for me?" he exclaimed. "I love it! Thank you, Shiloh. I'm going to put this in a frame in my house and put it on a shelf that I can see every time I go home. I really like my picture. I will see you again soon. Keep on coloring and make another picture for me, okay?" he asked.

She didn't respond, but he was okay with that. She gave him her picture and then she picked up the one he gave to her and held it in her hand. She didn't look his way, but he knew that the little bit of progress he'd made with her was a major milestone and he was happy.

"I'm going to leave and let Ms. Rose come in to get you. I will see you again really soon."

Cyrus looked toward the glass window and nodded just before heading toward the glass door to leave the room. Before closing the door behind him, he looked back again at Shiloh and was happy to see that she was no longer looking at the floor. She was looking at him and she was smiling and holding her picture in her hand. He waved and held up the picture she'd given him. When she gave him a slight wave, he felt tears well up in his eyes and for the first time in his entire life, he fell in love and if he never felt this way again, he would never forget this moment – not for *anything* in the world.

Entering the glass enclosed room where her foster mother was talking to Daniella, both women looked at him as if they were seeing a ghost.

"What?" he asked looking between the two of them.

"She colored with you. She gave you a picture. She looked and smiled at you. What are you, some kind of kid whisperer?" Daniella joked.

"She's my daughter and we had a vibe," he said.

"I think in thirty days, Judge Mathers will be impressed with you. I'm going to log this visit and make sure I highlight that interaction. No one will be able to doubt the connection you have with Shiloh," Daniella said.

"That child has been with me for over a month now and she'll color alone, but not once has she ever colored with me or even looked at me. She senses something with you," Rose said.

"I hope so because before I got here today, I didn't know what to expect. I didn't know how I was going to feel or what would happen, but as of this second, I know that I will go through hell and high water to get my daughter."

"That's good to hear because she needs you," Daniella said.

Cyrus nodded his head and looked at the picture in his hand of a princess colored in pink. He didn't know what was coming over him, but the first thing on his mind was to stop at a store to pick up a picture frame and then find out where he could get some hair ribbons, bows and flowers that little girls like in their hair. He was ready to do anything that would bring a smile to her face and have her look at him again. He looked between Daniella and Rose.

"More than that, before today, I didn't know it, but I need her too. Thank you for letting me see her today and for giving me that time with her. When is my first court appointed visit?" he asked.

"Do you want to do next week or the week after that?" Daniella asked.

"Next week on whatever day you say," he acknowledged.

Cyrus was excited. He was edgy like he needed to get out of the room and just move around. He needed to walk. His mind was all over the place with what he needed to do in order to prove himself to everyone who had a stake in the decision of where Shiloh goes. He knew he had an uphill battle ahead of him and he knew where he needed to start. He'd heard all the judge had to say and he needed a new game plan.

"Her sessions with the counselor are on Wednesdays at ten in the morning. Virginia traffic can be a beast, so you should get on the road very early to not miss your time with her which will start at noon after she gets a snack following her session. I have the information here in this folder that you'll need about where to go and what to do. I know you mentioned buying her some ribbons and stuff like that and small gifts are fine. I have a list of things Ms. Rose has already found that she likes. She seemed to liven up when you mentioned ribbons and bows for her hair. If you need me to get those for you, let me know and I'll have them for your next visit," Daniella offered.

"No, I'll take care of it. I have someone I can ask for help," he replied.

"That's great. I have also included information on recommendations for counselors for you to choose from in your area. That is required by the court, so please schedule those as soon as possible. Once a week for an hour is all that's required. Everything else you need to know from your appearance today is logged in the folder. If you have any questions, call me at any time. If you have questions for Ms. Rose about how Shiloh is doing in the interim, call me and I'll connect with her for you. Do you have any questions for either of us right now?" Daniella asked.

Cyrus looked at Shiloh through the window and saw that she was coloring another picture.

"I know you're doing your best and I appreciate you both. I remember my niece always being dressed in cute dresses and outfits just for little girls in bright colors. Can I buy her an outfit or two? I don't want to get too much stuff, but I would like to get a few things, if that's okay," he queried.

"That would actually be wonderful," Rose exclaimed happily. "I try to do what I can and when there is a parent involved, I do recommend that they do what they would like to do, just not so much because space for clothes for each child is limited. I think Shiloh would be stimulated more with pretty things. I will email her sizes to Daniella and she'll get that to you later today. Will that work?" Rose asked.

"Yes, ma'am. That would be perfect. Again, thanks to you both for all that you're doing and for finding me. I never would have abandoned her if I had known about her. I don't know why I was never told about her though she thought to list me on Shiloh's birth certificate. Now that I know, I'm not going anywhere and I will fight to make sure her life is better from this day forward. She's my kid," he said.

"She is and you know what? I think she feels a connection to you. No one, not even her counselor has been able to get her to look at them. She always looks down or looks away. In less than an hour, she looked at you, she smiled and she gave you a picture she painted and I caught that little wave she gave you. I'm amazed!" Daniella cheered.

Cyrus felt pretty good himself. Now, he had work to do and though counseling and parenting classes would be hard, his pride taking a hit was going to be the hardest, but he needed to do it; he had to do it. It wouldn't be an easy beginning back to his past, but it was a necessary one if he was ever going to get custody of his daughter. He had new priorities in life and he was looking at the main one on the other side of the glass window.

# 7

Marcus Jackson raced down the steps from the upstairs landing to the kitchen, skipping a few steps when he smelled bacon cooking and knew that Shamari, the woman he'd been madly in love with way before he asked her to marry him, must be having a good morning. It wasn't often she cooked bacon for him and the kids, especially on a school day. He often grabbed a breakfast sandwich on his way into the office and the kids would normally get a cold cereal of their choice. Shamari being off from work from the hospital today where she worked as an emergency room head nurse, was probably the reason why they were getting what he would call his breakfast for champions.

"Bacon, bacon, *bacon*!" he hollered walking up and turning her around to kiss her full on the lips with what he thought would be a quick kiss, but the moment her beautiful face came into view, he didn't want to let her luscious lips go.

"Someone is having a good morning," Shamari said pulling back.

Marcus kissed her quickly again and moved to the other side of the large island that sat six along the opposite side.

"More like someone got extra lucky last night. I mean, you put something on a brother and I'm still feeling it. I think I heard wolves howling outside of the bedroom window!" Marcus quipped.

When Shamari doubled over in laughter, he laughed out loud along with her.

"I think that was *you*!" she screamed.

"I'm almost tempted to stay home from the office today to spend the day in bed with you after the kids are off to school. I haven't done that in a while," he said.

"Not today, lover boy! I'm spending the day with my sister getting pampered from head to toe. Things have been so crazy at the hospital lately that by the time I get off, all I want to do is hug on the kids, love all on you and lay in the family room where we all watch anything as long as it's good time spent, especially with your wild schedule. I know your latest case is really dragging you. You know you can't take today off. You have to prepare for your closing remarks. I saw on the news that tomorrow is your big day. Are you ready?" she asked.

Marcus attempted to respond and then closed his

mouth when words wouldn't come. He wasn't sure if he was ready. His client, a black teenager, had been charged with attempted murder, though he didn't actually commit a crime, but was there when the crime occurred. As a lawyer, he spent his days fighting for the rights of everyone who came to him for help and this young man pricked his heart. The client, Jesse, reminded him of himself when he was sixteen years old. He hadn't been doing the right things and one day when he was faced with going to jail by following the wrong crowd, he changed everything about the direction his life was going and it was all because of a lawyer who worked to get him a second chance when he was faced with juvenile detention. Every day, he now worked to do that same thing for those the system wouldn't think twice about locking away and throwing the key down a drain. He wanted to make a difference and hoped he could with Jesse's case.

Looking up when Shamari placed a plate of bacon, scrambled eggs and buttered wheat toast in front of him, he exhaled and prepared to give her the answer she was waiting for.

"I am as ready as I can possibly be. The best part of this is I was able to convince his mother and other family members to come to court these last few days so that the judge and jury could see that he had family who is willing to help him turn his life around. I wouldn't be a lawyer today if it wasn't for a lawyer who fought for me. I'm going all in on my closing remarks and all I can do is hope and pray it works. I don't want to see another young man get lost in a system that's not built for him to succeed," he replied.

"Baby, he's lucky to have you and I know you're going to do fine," Shamari said.

Marcus looked around and realized he didn't hear or see Mariah and Carmelo, their seven and nine-year-old daughter and son.

"Where are the kids? They didn't smell this bacon and come running?" he asked in between bites of bacon and eggs that he slathered across his toast.

"Tyler's mom picked them up this morning for an early morning program at school. They both want to be in a play and the first rehearsal was this morning before school. They were so excited, they didn't want breakfast. They grabbed fruit and ran out when her van pulled up. I'm picking them all up later this afternoon since she dropped them off."

"Ah, you're playing carpool mom today. I hope you and your sister Maxine have a fun-filled day. If you need money, there's some in the drawer upstairs where I keep my watches. Take what you need," he said.

"I love you. You take such good care of me, but today, Maxine is treating. She's excited about a new guy in her life and wanted me to spend the day with her so that she could gush about him. With her footing the bill, I'm going to let her gush all day long!"

she laughed.

Marcus dived into his breakfast, checking the time though he knew he didn't have to rush. He didn't have anything going on at the law firm until around ten. As he ate, he checked email on his iPad.

"I'm hoping to get home early tonight," he said.

"Oh, that would be great. I know you've had a lot of late nights lately. Do you know where my iPad is? I know I had it last night," Shamari asked.

"Check the living room sofa. You left it in the family room and I put it in the living room so that you'd see it when you came downstairs this morning."

Marcus watched his sexy wife as she walked by him in a pink and black sweat suit with a white apron tied around her waist. The best day of his life was the day he turned eighteen and met her at a hot dog stand on the campus of Howard University where she was a nursing student and he was diving into undergraduate law classes.

"I see it," Shamari shouted back at him.

"Good. We need to sync our schedules for vacation time this summer. We promised the kids a trip to Disney World in Orlando and I want to be sure I put in the time early and you'll need to do the same thing. I was thinking about the two weeks right after they get out of school. What do you think about that?" Marcus asked.

Finishing up his breakfast, he was surprised when Shamari didn't answer. At thirty-five, he didn't think she was having a senior moment and hadn't paid attention to what he said. Turning around from the counter, he leaned to the side to look from the kitchen through the dining room in order to see her standing in the living room. What he saw caused him to stop chewing and turn around in his seat.

"Marcus?" Shamari hollered.

"Baby, what's wrong?" he asked.

Marcus knew something had to be wrong when he saw her standing stoic and emotionless in front of the large bay window as she looked between him and the window, back at him and then again to the window. He jumped up and rushed to see what had caused her to get so quiet with an alarmed look on her face. When he reached her, he looked out of the window and saw what she saw and now, he joined her in a moment of being shocked. Were his eyes playing tricks on him?

"Is that Cyrus?" Shamari asked pointing out of the window.

Marcus knew exactly who it was. There was no question about who he saw pacing back and forth in front of the house as if he was contemplating whether to come up to the house or get back in his shiny new black truck. The windows were all as dark as the truck's color and it glistened like he'd just rolled off the car lot with it.

"What do you think is going on with him? I can't believe he's actually out there," Shamari said.

Before the words even left her mouth, Marcus had

been thinking the same thing. He hadn't seen his brother in two years, if not longer than that.

Cyrus lived in Washington, D.C. while he and his family made their home in Montgomery County in Maryland, in an affluent neighborhood. They may be brothers, but their lives were like night and day. While he eventually became a lawyer, Cyrus chose to let the streets control his life. He wasn't sure if Cyrus was still heavily involved in illegal activity as he has been known to be involved in. He never expected to look outside to find him pacing back and forth as if the weight of the world was on his shoulders and he didn't know where to go. He must be torn if he got up early in the morning and drove to end up here. He'd heard some talk about his brother and being a lawyer, he was able to keep a subtle eye on him. So far, he was sure Cyrus wasn't on the up and up, but he hadn't been arrested on anything and that was good considering the nature of his past.

"I don't know," Marcus replied.

"How long has it been?" Shamari asked.

"I think at least two years. The last time I saw him, we got into that big blowout over his criminal activity and the impact it could have on the family," Marcus said as his eyes stayed on Cyrus who still hadn't made a move to come to the front door. "That was the week after his father's funeral and he came by here. He was still so angry and I was trying to calm him down when it got out of control," Marcus explained.

"Right, he came to the funeral, but stayed in the back and left before the ceremony was over. Was that really the last time?" she inquired.

"Yeah because that next week was Mariah's fifth birthday party and he didn't show up, but he sent bags and bags of gifts, especially that life-size princess doll that she still cherishes. I tried with him," Marcus admitted.

Marcus felt Shamari's hand caressing his back, soothing where she knew he was tightening up in anticipation of why his brother would show up after all this time.

"Baby, I know you did and whatever is going on with him, it must be serious if he's at our house."

Marcus turned to Shamari.

"Maybe he's here to see you. I know you and he were in contact after he stopped talking to me," he said.

"Well, we'll never know if he doesn't come to the door or if one of us doesn't go outside. I vote that it be you. I know you and Cyrus have never seen eye to eye because of how he chose to live his life and make his money, but he's still your brother and for some reason, he's here," Shamari said.

Marcus contemplated and tried to think of a reason Cyrus would come to see him after so many years. It couldn't be an issue with their mother because he talked to her at least once a week and she always asked him about Cyrus which meant, she hadn't heard from him either.

"I'm going to go out and see what's going on," Marcus said. "If I don't, he may get back in his truck and drive off thinking coming here was a mistake."

"I think that's the right thing to do and don't make him feel horrible about coming here after no contact for two years. We're family and family sticks together no matter what. Something must be really wrong, though I hate to say that because he should be able to come to us when things are going good too. Right now, I'll take what we can get. I miss Cy and I know the kids miss him too. He still sends gifts on their birthdays and holidays, but I know they wish he would be around more," Shamari offered.

"I know. It's my fault that we're estranged, right? It's because I push him or he feels like I put him down or compare him to me, but I don't. Do I?" Marcus asked her and turned to face her.

"You don't, but he can't help how he feels when he knows the two of you took two different paths. I don't care what path he's on or what he has done or is doing, he's still your brother and we love him. I'm going to go clean up the kitchen from breakfast. I'll keep my eye out for any bloodshed. You and your brother are like a cat and a dog who don't like each other and while you bite, he'll scratch and neither of you will win."

Marcus chuckled.

"Thanks for at least making me the dog in that fight. Whew!" he shouted as he headed toward the front door.

"You'll always be top dog in my book, now go see what's bothering your brother," Shamari said.

Marcus watched her walk away and he took a deep breath to prepare for whatever Cyrus was about to lay on him.

The minute he opened the door, Marcus expected Cyrus to at least look his way, but he didn't. He continued to pace on the sidewalk at the end of the driveway. This must be bad, he thought. Maybe Cyrus was in legal trouble again and this time, he was coming for help instead of pushing his brother, the lawyer, away.

"Cy?" Marcus uttered when he was close enough that Cyrus could hear him without him shouting.

This time Cyrus did look his way and Marcus knew that Shamari shouldn't expect any bloodshed. Something was wrong and it had nothing to do with him. He saw a look on Cyrus' face that he'd never seen before. Cyrus was scared.

He watched his brother place his hands inside of the pants pockets of the black sweat suit he was wearing and with no emotion, Cyrus looked him dead in the eyes the moment he walked right up to him. Marcus didn't attempt to hug him or greet him in any kind of way. He had already decided he would let Cyrus dictate their interaction.

"Hey, Marc. I guess you're surprised to see me, huh?" Cyrus asked.

"I am, but it's a good surprise. We've all missed you, especially the kids," Marcus said.

"I send them gifts on holidays and for their birthdays," Cyrus explained.

"You do, but they miss you and so do I. Are you okay? Do you want to come inside?" Marcus asked.

"I..I..don't know yet. I mean, I've been up since around three in the morning and I've been driving back and forth through your neighborhood for almost an hour. I finally stopped because I think in a few minutes, a few of your neighbors were going to call the police after seeing me drive back and forth," Cyrus joked.

"Yeah, they would have done that. There are times I feel like I have to convince them that I live here when they see me," Marcus kidded. "Now, back to you. What's going on? Is everything alright?"

He waited and noticed Cyrus struggling with sharing as he was known to do. There was a time when they were close when they were kids, but that all ended when Cyrus started hanging out with a rough crowd just before he, himself left for college, leaving Cyrus in North Carolina with their mother. Rather than force a conversation, he stood with Cyrus and waited until he was ready to talk. Seconds later, Cyrus turned toward him.

"I have a daughter."

Marcus wasn't sure he heard him.

"Come again? Did you say you have a daughter? What? When? Where? Was she just born?" Marcus questioned.

"No. She's five," Cyrus offered.

"Five! Why am I just hearing about this? Why haven't you told me before now?"

"I just found out about her. I messed around with this girl a few years ago that I met while down at Virginia Beach. Things happened and she never told me about her."

Marcus rubbed his hand down his face trying to take in the fact that his baby brother, though thirty-two-years old, had a kid.

"What's her name and where is she?" Marcus asked.

"Her name is Shiloh and right now, she's in foster care. It's a long story and I mean a very long one."

Marcus exhaled and knew that just hearing the words that his brother had a kid was going to be a long story.

"Let's go inside the house and get some coffee," Marcus said.

"You have time? You're not on your way to work? I was going to stop earlier, but I was trying to get my thoughts together and I didn't know if I was welcomed here after that blowout we had two years ago after the funeral," Cyrus said as they walked toward the front door.

"I do, but I'll send a message that I'll be late. I have court, but not until around noon. And you're always welcome here. You're my brother. I never told you that you weren't welcomed here. You decided to stay away. I tried calling you several times back then and you ignored me," Marcus said.

"I know. I was angry. I was mad angry back then, especially after, you know who died. He was a horrible man and I never should have gone to his funeral. Going only made me angrier. When I came over here a week later, I felt like you were judging me," Cyrus said.

"I wasn't doing that and I would never do that. I know the man your father was and I know the things he did to you, the things mom allowed him to do to you, but that's in the past. Let's not go back there. Right now, you have a kid and I want to hear about her and find out why she's in foster care," Marcus said.

Once inside the house, Marcus moved to the side as Shamari came running toward them with lightning speed and launched herself into Cyrus' outstretched arms.

"Oh, my goodness! I have missed you so much!" she screamed.

"I've missed you too, sis! You look amazing. You're still hanging in there with this guy?" Cyrus joked.

"Yeah, after one kid in, I could have escaped, but

after the second, I kind of had to stick around and make it work," Shamari laughed.

"I'm right here!" Marcus yelled as Cyrus put Shamari back down on her feet.

"Are the kids here or already gone to school?" Cyrus asked.

"They're already at school with before school programs. How have you been? You look good, so I assume you're doing good?"

"I'm doing great, Sis."

"Come on into the kitchen and I'll get you both some coffee. Are you hungry? Do you want something to eat?" Shamari asked.

"No, I'm good. I just came to talk and get some advice – some legal advice," Cyrus admitted.

"Everything okay?" Shamari asked and stopped moving around.

Marcus looked to Cyrus who looked to him as if to say he wanted someone else to tell her why he was visiting. Marcus gave in and decided to help him out.

"He's got a kid – a little girl who is five-years-old and right now, in foster care. That's pretty much all I got so far, oh, and her name is Shiloh," Marcus explained.

"What! She's five? Why are we just hearing about her? Why is she in foster care?" Shamari asked.

"Mari, let the man sit and I'm sure he'll explain," Marcus said taking a seat at the island in one of the six chairs.

"Oh, sorry," she said.

"That's okay. I knew it would be a shock. It was for me when I found out. I'll try and cut through most of what we don't need to talk about right at this moment and get to the important part."

Marcus sat down as Shamari made coffee for them all.

"We're all ears," Marcus said.

"Okay, as I told you outside, I didn't know about Shiloh until recently. I met her mother years ago, things happened and she had Shiloh and never told me. I will say that I'm not sure she knew how to find me after that weekend, though she did have my name and information on the club I'd just opened up back then," he explained.

"Where is her mother?" Shamari asked, sitting coffee in front of them along with cream and sugar from the white kitchen cabinet.

"She's dead. All I know is that there was some kind of police chase and Brenda, that's Shiloh's mother, and another guy who was driving were killed when the car went over a steep embankment. A friend told the police about me and not long ago a woman from child services in Virginia paid me a visit with this story that I may be a father. I took a paternity test and it came back that I am the father," Cyrus said, trying imitate Maury from the popular television show where establishing paternity was made a mockery of.

"So, she ended up in foster care after the crash

that killed her mother. Was she in the car?" Marcus asked.

"No. She was with someone else who then took her to the police when she heard about the accident and realized she didn't know what to do with Shiloh. Now, the crazy part. After I find out I'm the father and that actually sank in, I had to go to court and this judge raked me over the coals, but I admit, I deserved it. They recommended I seek representation and I didn't do that. I went in, sort of like I look now, but with a lot more bling and she pretty much told me that based on my history and what she knew about my life now, though there is no proof, she doubted I was worthy to be Shiloh's father. Everyone in that courtroom looked at me like I was trash. She's my kid and I understand her mother was into drugs and all kinds of other things. Shiloh is five and she's all alone. I was able to see her and I swear, you know how you've always said if you weren't secure in your marriage, you would think that Mariah was my kid because she looks like me?" Cyrus asked.

Marcus laughed. He had joked about that since Mariah was about two and looked so much like Cyrus that it was scary.

"Yeah?"

"Shiloh looks like she could be Mariah's twin. She's got the same long, thick black hair. She has light brown eyes like you, me and Mariah. She is so beautiful. I saw her through a window before I got the chance to be in the room with her to talk to her and she looked like she was so alone. It ate away at my heart, a heart I didn't know I had. You know how hardnosed I can be, but not when I saw my daughter sitting in a corner like she didn't think anybody cared about her. I wanted to get her out of there and bring her home. I gotta get her out of there, Marc. I need your help. I need to get my daughter out of there. She's in foster care like she doesn't have any family, but she has me," Cyrus said.

"And she has us," Shamari added.

"Damn right, she has us," Marcus chimed in loudly.

"When can we see her?" Shamari asked.

"Whoa, wait a minute. That's not how this works," Marcus said.

"He's right. I have scheduled visitation for one hour that will be supervised and the judge gave me some harsh walking orders. My first visit in Virginia is in two days. I need to come correct for my next court date in November. Until then, I have these supervised visits all the way in Virginia, which is not a problem. I talked to Shiloh for a little bit and I swear, I don't know who that guy was. We talked, or I talked about hair and princesses and pink stuffed toys. I tapped into my time with Mariah over the years and I was a different person. That person wants his daughter out of foster care and I need your help. I have to have counseling and take parenting classes and a bunch of other requirements in this paperwork they gave me."

When Cyrus stopped talking, Marcus took that moment to speak.

"Where's the paperwork? I need to see it to see what is required and let me just say this so that you know what to expect. Simply because you are Shiloh's father does not mean the court will give you custody at any stage of the process. They are going to dig deep into your life to see what crawls out. Anything we need to be concerned about?" Marcus asked.

"Of course, there is, but is there anything they can find? I doubt it. I've learned how to cover myself though law enforcement has tried, unsuccessfully. My people are loyal to me. I know what you mean though and I'm already all over that. I know I have to change some things and I will. I just need to know what to do that's right and not screw this up. Before knowing about Shiloh, my life was one way, but now that I know about her, all I want to do is make her the one and only priority and prove to the court that what they think about me based on what's in their files and what they see is not all there is to me – not now that I've met my daughter and I see how much she needs me. I just need you and Shamari to help me. Tell me what I need to do in order to get my daughter out of foster care. I know it won't happen overnight, but I want it to happen. I want my daughter. I've never felt the need to change for anyone, but for her, the moment I saw her little cute face, I would give my life to make sure she was out of that system."

"Cy, we are with you all the way and I can't wait to meet my niece. Wait until Mariah and Carmelo hear about her. I'm so happy for you," Shamari said.

"I am too," Marcus added.

"You're not pissed I showed up asking for help out of the blue?" Cyrus asked.

"Not one bit. We're family and I don't care what brought you back to us. Promise me that no matter what, you won't disappear like that on us again or ignore us again. We should always be able to work out any issues and now that there is a little girl involved, I think Shamari would kill you if you tried to keep her away from us and trust me, I would help her hide the body!" Marcus joked.

"I hear you. Think I have any chance? I know we're not addressing the elephant in the room, that is my lifestyle, but I need you to know that Shiloh is the only priority."

"Cy, you will definitely have a chance. I'm going to represent you and we're going to get my niece out of the system. Remember, it will take some time and you have to walk a straight line. Any demons following you around, now is the time to get rid of them. The court will have the final say over where Shiloh goes and she needs to be with our family, not with strangers. You have to follow my advice, follow my lead or this won't work. You ready to do that?" Marcus asked.

"Bro, I'm ready to do anything. You didn't see her.

When you do, you will see what I mean. She's all me and I need her to know she has somebody. She has me," Cyrus declared.

"And me," Shamari shouted.

"And me!" Marcus yelled.

# 8 CHAPTER NAME

Cyrus sat nervously in the waiting room of the counseling service, waiting for Shiloh's session to end. His leg shook nervously in anticipation of seeing his daughter again. In the chair beside him sat a bag of things that Shamari helped him pick out after she cancelled her plans with her sister and instead, took him to various stores where she often shopped for Mariah.

Inside the bag, there was a pretty long-sleeved pink and white casual dress that they picked out together. Since it was October, Shamari told him he needed to get things that were weather appropriate. They'd also picked out a nice pink winter coat since the temperature was changing with each day. There was also a denim outfit complete with jeans and a jacket to match with a picture of a princess on the back of the jacket and on the back pockets of the jeans. As promised, he'd also picked up lots of ribbons, colorful balls, headbands with flowers on them and barrettes for her hair. The idea of having them seemed to bring her enjoyment when he brought it up and so he made sure he got them in various colors. He'd also picked up a few coloring books and a new box of crayons. He also bought three books that Shamari recommended. He wanted to use this visit and read a book or two to her. Shamari made him look at videos on YouTube that showed how to read a book to a child with excitement to engage them. He wasn't sure he'd get much of a reaction from Shiloh, but he would do anything he needed to do in hopes that he could. He didn't think so during his first visit with her and she surprised him. This was the first of many visits and though he wanted to do everything on his first visit, Shamari and Marcus had to talk him back from the ledge. Even they couldn't believe the excitement he had over having a daughter.

After leaving the courthouse the week before, he told Jason all about his visit with Shiloh and the things he was being required to do. They also talked about the judge's admonishment of how he showed up in court blinged out with no support system and with lots of self-doubt and hesitation, he told Jason of his plan to put pride aside and reach out to his brother.

The day he showed up at Marcus' house, it took a while for him to go inside, thinking Marcus would make him grovel, but that was far from what happened. He and Shamari have been nothing but supportive in helping him with what he needed, including Marcus agreeing to being his attorney of record and the promise that the four of them, including his niece and nephew, would be with him for his next court day in a month. Though Marcus suggested he reach to their mother for support, Cyrus wasn't ready for that conversation. There was so much bad blood between the two of them, that he wasn't sure they would be able to get over their troubles to have her stand with him to support him in court. She would probably do it, but he wasn't sure he wanted her there – at least not yet. He had enough to deal with and drama with his mother wasn't at the top of his list. He had a lot to do, according to Marcus.

One thing that he hadn't thought about was, if he were to get custody of Shiloh, there was no way the place where he lived now would be approved. The judge had already made reference to it and he was shocked that she even knew about his condo. He'd gone through great trouble to conceal his ownership of it.

He lived on the top floor, penthouse of a new condominium complex in D.C. The place was nice, but without Marcus even seeing it, his brother told him of all of the things the court would find wrong with the condo starting with the party atmosphere he knew Cyrus lived in daily. Cyrus thought about his place and the all black theme in all of the rooms. When you entered the three-bedroom condo, there was an open floor layout in colors of black and gray. His bedroom was painted in dark gray with black furniture. One of the bedrooms he knew would secure that he would never get his daughter was the room painted in red with all black furniture and was made for all of his sexual escapades and wild parties from the swing that descended from one corner of the room, and it wasn't a swing for children, to the stripper poles in that room, the main family room and in his bedroom. He lived the life of a bachelor and wasn't ashamed of it, but now taking on the role of a father, he needed to make a serious change.

He often played loud music and there were non-child appropriate movies that blared from the large screen televisions that were placed in every room. Each room had its own bar and during any given week, he hosted two to three parties, most times with a group of his friends and often times with him and the woman of the moment. He didn't have to tell Marcus about his place for him to know what it consisted of. Thankful to his brother, he decided to begin the search for a new house and was hoping to have one that wasn't too far from Marcus and Shamari since they offered to help with Shiloh, something the judge was going to check for during his next court visit in a month. Money wasn't an object when it came to making sure he had the kind of home that would be conducive to raising a young girl. He would keep his place in D.C., but his main residence would be where he would plan to have a room decorated just for Shiloh. He assumed before any real decision was made for permanency when it came to where Shiloh would live, he would be allowed to have her overnight, perhaps for a night or two. If that were the case, he needed to be prepared with a place that would pass an inspection by Shiloh's case worker and with the court's permission. He didn't think it would happen before Thanksgiving, which was coming up in a few weeks, but he was hoping he would be able to bring her to spend time with his family over Christmas. He didn't know how long the process would be, but in doing all the right things, he was hoping to get Shiloh out of foster care and around family. His niece and nephew were already excited about meeting her. He was still at their how when they arrived home from school. When he and Shamari were done shopping, he dropped her off at their house and she insisted that he wait inside until she returned so that the kids could see him.

His phone vibrated in his pocket, shaking him from thoughts of the week before. Seeing the number, he left the bag on the seat and stepped out of the office into the hallway.

"What's up Bruno?" he asked, answering.

"Boss, you have a shipment coming through the club tonight and we need to get it to one of the houses. Where do you want it delivered? Also, Oscar is asking about your next shipment. I told him you've been busy when he asked why you haven't been at either of the clubs over the weekend or this week or even the recording studio in over a week. What should I tell him?" Bruno asked.

Cyrus hadn't been focused on business since his court date. His days and nights have been focused on what he needed to do to convince the judge he could take care of Shiloh and in the midst of that, he put business to the side.

"I can't deal with that right now. Handle the shipment and take it to either of the three houses, it doesn't matter. Tell Oscar, no shipments for a while. I don't have time right now for any of this. I'm dealing with some personal stuff that he doesn't need to know about and you should work with Jason to get business taken care of," Cyrus explained.

He heard Bruno expel a loud breath on the other end.

"Oscar isn't going to like that. You move the most weight for him and he's not going to like taking in less money with an explanation that you're busy."

"I don't owe Oscar any explanation for how I run my business. He can find another source and right now, he doesn't have a choice."

"Will you be at the club tonight? We're expecting a huge crowd tonight and I think Oscar is planning to come through to talk to you," Bruno asked.

"I'm out of town and I won't be back until tomorrow. I'm staying the night in a hotel because I'll be here late. Like I said, check with Jason on what you need," Cyrus explained.

"Out of town? Where?" Bruno asked.

Cyrus hadn't told anyone about Shiloh other than Jason and he'd rather keep everyone in the dark for now.

"Just out of town. Jason will be there and he can handle Oscar if he needs to connect with someone."

"Boss, I can handle it if you tell me what's going on. Oscar may be too much for Jason to deal with. I'm not sure he could go toe-to-toe with Oscar and his men. Let me take care of it. Bring me up to speed with what's going on and let me handle it," Bruno suggested. "Jason doesn't have to be the only one on the team you lean to. I can handle things better than he can," Bruno added.

Cyrus liked that Bruno was ready to do whatever was asked of him, but Bruno was too eager and he and Jason were both developing trust issues when it came to Bruno. On more than one occasion, Cyrus believed that Bruno had an ulterior motive to begin making his own deals to undercut the current operation. He needed to keep an eye on him and the last thing he wanted was for Bruno to have any inside information that could hurt the enterprise.

"Nah, let Jason handle it. He'll be fine. He knows what's going on and what to do."

Cyrus was about to continue when the door to the office opened and the receptionist signaled for him to come back in.

"I'm telling you that Oscar won't respect you if you let Jason handle this for you. You have never not been available for him. It should be me handling this if you need to be away and you know it," Bruno stated.

"You're thinking for me now?" Cyrus shouted a little louder than he'd planned. "Don't push me, Bruno. You won't like the outcome. This is my business and I know what I'm doing and I know who I want to speak for me when I'm not around and when I say it's Jason, it's Jason. Are we clear?" he asked sternly, making sure his point wasn't questioned again.

"I hear you. Do you want to at least tell me where you are? You may need me for something, especially if it's business related," Bruno said.

Cyrus was now pissed. Bruno was fishing and he didn't like it.

"I'll be back tomorrow, so follow the instructions I gave and that's all you need to know. I'm out. Reach to Jason with anything you need. I'll be unreachable until I return tomorrow. Jason knows how to reach me if it's important. Clear?" he asked in a demanding voice.

"Clear, Boss."

Cyrus hung up and turned his phone off before heading back into the office.

"Is she done?" he asked the receptionist.

"Yes, she is. Give us a minute to get her settled in

the visitation room and then you can go in. She's finishing up her snack. Her caseworker is here and wants to speak to you. She'll be right out."

"Thanks," Cyrus said and rather than sit back down, he paced back and forth in front of the chair he was sitting in. He was nervous, something he never experienced with business, but in dealing with his own daughter, he was nervous. He hoped she would like the things he brought for her and more than anything, he hoped she would look his way again and maybe this time, even say a word or two. He'd been thinking about her for a whole week, anxious to get back to her.

"Mr. Jackson?"

Cyrus turned around as Daniella entered the room through a door on the side of the room.

"Hi," he responded.

"It's good to see you again and I see you brought gifts," she said. "Do you mind if I take a look before you go in?" she asked.

"Oh, not at all," Cyrus said, handing the bag to her. He watched as she took out one thing after the other.

"These are very nice," she said.

"Is it too much?" he asked.

"No, not at all. They're very pretty," she said putting everything back and handing the bag back to him. "I also received the email that you've set up your sessions. I understand you went with a counselor here in Richmond?" she asked.

"I did. I figured since I was going to be here every Wednesday to see Shiloh that I would stay the night before to make sure I'm here and on time and then after my visit, I scheduled my own session with a counselor and he's only a few miles from here. I have a two-hour break after my visits with Shiloh."

When Daniella smiled, Cyrus felt like he was on the right track.

"You're full of surprises. You also mentioned you were going to buy a house in a nice family-orientated neighborhood? You're a little ahead of the game," she said.

"I know, but I didn't want to do it at the last minute. My brother and his wife are helping me. He's an attorney and he knows a lot about the system. He's also going to represent me from this point forward to make sure I don't do anything stupid like show up in court with all of my platinum again or looking like I just came from performing at a rap concert," he joked.

When Daniella laughed, he felt the tension ease from his body. He worked hard at building his empire, even through illegal means, but what he was going through to get his daughter was the hardest thing in his life that he's had to do.

"You reached to family?" she asked. "Good move. The judge will love that. Does he have any children around Shiloh's age?" she inquired.

"Yes. They have a daughter who is seven and a son

who is nine and they are both excited about meeting Shiloh one day," he explained.

"Perhaps the judge will consider a family visit. I'll make note of that in my file. Family is always good in these situations. Are you ready to see Shiloh?" she asked.

"Yes."

"Just like before, you'll be in a play room full of toys and books, but this time, Shiloh will be in the room alone – there are no other children in there. I'll be on the other side of the room, still allowing you space with her to have your visit since your visits have to be supervised. You'll have two hours this week and next week. If those go well, I've requested extra time for your last two visits before we go back to court. Your last visit is during the week of Thanksgiving and Ms. Rose is planning a dinner the day before Thanksgiving allowing the parents to come in and have dinner with their kids. If you want, that dinner can take the place of your weekly visit. You'll have much more time than the usual allotted time. Some don't show up, but if you want to, you're invited. I did get that cleared by the judge and she stated she's only agreeing to it if your three visits prior to that go well."

Cyrus lit up. He wasn't expecting that. He had been invited to dinner with his brother and his family for Thanksgiving Day and he had already begun feeling out of place thinking of Shiloh having Thanksgiving in a foster home. Dinner the day before is something and he would take it.

"I would love that. Should I bring something?" he asked.

"Let me email Rose and ask her and I'll forward her email to you. How's that?" she asked.

"That's perfect. Can I see Shiloh now?" he asked and wasn't shy about how excited he was.

Daniella laughed and he laughed with her. She probably thought he was a nut.

"Never lose that excitement over seeing your daughter. It will go a long way to her being more comfortable with you. I wanted to talk to you briefly to let you know something. Her counselor today told her that you're her father. Shiloh still hasn't talked to her, but she's a good listener," she said.

"She did? Was there any reaction?" he asked.

"None. She said she told her about the man she met whose name was Cyrus. She explained that though her mother had gone to heaven, we were able to find her father. She explained that you didn't know about her and that's why you're around now because we were able to locate you. She asked her how she felt about meeting her dad and she didn't react. I wanted you to know so that when you go in with her, you know that she knows who you are even if she doesn't say anything. Keep that in mind as you're talking to her and it's okay to tell her that she's your daughter and how happy you are about that. I know this is all new to you, so if you need me, just signal if you need me and I'll intervene. After the visit, I'll leave with her while you're still in the room. Let her leave first and then you can leave. You have my number if you need to reach to me. I'm going to take her back to Rose and then I have other clients I need to visit, but if you have questions while you're still here, let me know. We good?" Daniella asked.

"Yes, and now I think I'm even more nervous with her knowing I'm her dad. I don't know if she will like that or not. I'm thirty-two and I still have resentment over my father not being around when I was younger, but then again, him being absent was a good thing," he bemoaned.

"Don't worry about it. Her counselor thought it was best to break that news to her to explain your weekly visits with her. Trust me, it's a good thing. Again, I'll be around if you need me or if she looks like she needs a break. Don't worry. If she reacts negatively in some way, don't react. Let me handle her, okay?" she asked.

"I got you. You're in charge and I like that. I'm still learning," Cyrus admitted.

"You're doing great. You're doing better than most and it's because I can tell your desire to do right by her comes from your heart and that's important. Follow me and don't forget your bag," Daniella stated.

Cyrus had already begun walking behind her and when she mentioned the bag, he remembered he sat it back on the seat after she looked through it.

"Got it," he said.

When they walked through one hallway and then another, they came to a room with a large, light-brown door. Cyrus inhaled deeply and prepared himself to see his daughter again. He was still getting used to hearing himself say he had a child.

"Ready?" she asked.

Cyrus nodded and followed her in. Shiloh wasn't sitting on the floor, but at a kids' table that sat in the middle of the room. She was already coloring when he walked in and she didn't look his way. He walked over to her and took a seat at the little table to sit across from her. He would endure days of being uncomfortable at the kiddie table if it made her feel comfortable being around him.

"Hi, Shiloh. Do you remember me from last week? My name is Cyrus. How are you today?" he asked, keeping his eyes on her though he didn't expect her to look his way.

"You're my dad," she said.

Cyrus almost fell out of his chair. He turned to Daniella who looked as shocked as he knew he looked to her. Neither were expecting a word from her let alone a couple of words.

He turned back around to not lose his immediate engagement with her.

"Yes, I am. Is that okay with you?" he asked.

Shiloh did respond with words, but hunched her shoulders.

"Well, okay, I guess it's not a bad thing then. My full name is Cyrus DeMarcus Jackson. I know that's a lot. I heard your full name is Shiloh Antonia Johnson. That's a pretty name for a little girl. I see you're already coloring. Can I color with you again today?" he asked.

He waited as Shiloh reached into the big box of crayons and handed him a blue crayon before going back to coloring.

"How did you know I like blue? I even have on a blue shirt today," Cyrus said, pointing to himself. For a second, Shiloh looked his way and then she quickly looked back at the coloring book. "I'll use it to color in one of these books here on the table. Should I pick one or do you want to pick one you want me to color? I want to color one you'll like that you can take with you again," he said.

When she didn't react, he reached for a book and then stopped when she reached over and grabbed a different one for him and pushed it across the table to him.

"Good choice," he said. " I see you're coloring with pink again. I guess I was right in thinking that you really liked pink. I bought you a few things and they all have pink on them. Do you want to see?" he asked.

Shiloh nodded and put her crayon down, but kept her eye on the book.

Cyrus sat the bag on the floor, reached inside and pulled out the pink dress first. He laid it out on the table and waited.

"First, there is this dress. Someone helped me pick this out saying that it's one a little girl who liked pink would like. Then there is this outfit in blue denim that has pink on the back and on the pockets. Do you like it?" he asked laying the outfit out on the table too. He was about to reach in the bag again when he saw Shiloh reach for the pink dress as she pulled it closer to her.

"Pretty," she whispered softly.

"Yes, it is and it's going to be pretty on you when you wear it one day."

"This pink too," she said pointing to the picture of a black princess imprinted on the back.

"It is. Do you like it?" he asked.

She nodded again, this time so vigorously that her braids bounced against the side of her face.

"Then I did good. I told you last time that I would bring you some pretty stuff for your hair and I have a few things in the bag. Do you want to take them out yourself?" he asked, moving the bag so that it was closer to her. He smiled when she reached for the bag and reached inside. As she pulled one hair decoration out after another, her excitement grew with each new thing. When she pulled out the two books of stories about princesses, he smiled when she handed him one.

"Can you read this one?" she asked him and then went back to the bag to see what else was in it.

"I can do that."

Cyrus quickly looked to Daniella who was writing away, probably in amazement at Shiloh's reaction to him. She kept telling him that everyone was having a hard time getting more than a word or two from Shiloh and yet, here she was practically having a conversation with him. If Shiloh wasn't excited, he was excited enough for them both.

He opened the book and began reading, taking his time from one page to the other. When he looked up, he saw Shiloh attempting to put some of the barrettes in her hair.

"You like those?" he asked her.

She nodded and continued to try and open the pack to put them in her hair. He turned to Daniella and mouthed his question silently.

"Can I help her?" he asked.

Daniella nodded yes and he moved a little closer, careful to move slowly in case Shiloh wasn't ready for that.

"Here, let me help you," he said.

She handed him the pack and in the next second, she not only looked up at him, but held his attention with her eyes without looking away.

He opened the pack and though he wasn't sure what to do, he fumbled around and found the snap to open. Reaching for her hair, he placed one pink one in the shape of Minnie Mouse at the end of one long braid and then one in white in the same shape on another.

"Wow, you look beautiful. I have a mirror on my phone. Do you want to see what it looks like?" he asked her.

"Yes," Shiloh said softly.

Cyrus quickly pulled out his phone and looked for the mirror app. Opening it, he turned it toward her and smiled when she lit up with a bright smile when she saw herself.

"You can keep all of these if you want. I thought you would like them. Should I start the book?" he asked.

"Yes," she answered, this time a little louder than before.

"You know, Shiloh, people thought you couldn't talk because you never say much. You can talk and you talk pretty good and strong. Why won't you talk to other people?" Cyrus asked.

"Mommy told me not to talk to, uh, um, I forget," Shiloh said looking up at him.

Cyrus smiled, enjoying the growth of their interaction.

"Strangers?" he asked.

Shiloh vigorously shook her head at him.

"But you talked to me. I was a stranger," he said.

"You my dad," she said quickly.

"Dads are okay?" he asked.

"My dad is. Mommy said so."

"Your mommy told you about your dad? About

me?" he asked.

"Yes. Mommy said one day my dad would come and I can talk to him."

Cyrus sat back bewildered. Brenda told Shiloh about him, but never told him she existed. He needed to know more.

"Did your mommy say where I was? Where your dad was at?" he asked.

"Far away, but when I got big, I could see him."

"Well, you're a pretty big girl and I'm glad I can see you now and I hope I get to see you all the time. Would you like that?" he asked.

When Shiloh smiled, he smiled back at her as she nodded yes and then pointed to the book. Cyrus laughed out loud. He guessed he was already discovering who was going to be in charge in their relationship. His daughter was already wrapping him around her finger.

To his amazement, Shiloh slid from her chair and sat in the chair right next to him, bringing them closer together. He went back to reading her a story about a little princess and he turned the book so that she could follow along with him. This visit went beyond his expectation. There was no turning back now. He wouldn't even if he could. Shiloh knew he was her dad and that was a hurdle he was happy to have surpassed.

# 9 CHAPTER NAME

*Club CyEmp* was jumping for a Tuesday night. Though the weekends were usually packed to the limit allowed by law, the crowd was still pretty steady throughout the week also, thanks to the happy hour Sunday through Wednesday nights. With Cyrus out of town again for the third week in a row handling his personal business, Jason sat behind Cyrus desk in his office and kept his eye on the business.

He and Cyrus had been friends since back in the day when Cyrus would save him from neighborhood bullies. Having no place to go after leaving his life in North Carolina as a sixteen-year-old and moving to the D.C. area thinking he could live with his brother, Cyrus slept on the floor of Jason's bedroom, for over a year without his mother knowing about it. When she finally found out, Jason thought his mother would throw Cyrus out, but she didn't. She allowed him to stay with them and after his mother died, Cyrus looked after him like family, bringing him into the drug game knowing that he could trust him with his life. Jason had been by Cyrus' side as a partner and best friend for years and now with Cyrus preoccupied, he had to step his game up and hold things down.

Jason liked that Cyrus kept his circle small, but that also meant that a lot fell on him when Cyrus needed someone to handle business.

Besides him, there were several other guys and the one closest to the both was the guy who started out as the muscle of the crew, Bruno. It had only been a few weeks since Cyrus has been preoccupied and he's noticed that Bruno has become more aggressive about his role in the organization, only stepping to him, never stepping to Cyrus when he was around. Kelly, at the front door already signaled to him that Bruno was on his way up and he was prepared for him. He may be short in stature compared to Bruno and Cyrus, but he still didn't take much mess and just to be safe, he removed his gun from the duffle bag he'd brought in with him and placed it on his lap under the desk. He wouldn't put it past Bruno to try and flex while Cyrus was away. He'd already gotten word that Bruno was trying to push his way to the top, making connections think that Cyrus was putting more trust in him when it came to business, something that was far from the truth.

He looked up just as Bruno came through the office door. Jason forgot he had a key and didn't feel comfortable with him having one anymore. He'd been told that while he was with helping with some business that Cyrus needed done the week before, that Bruno had made himself comfortable during the day behind Cyrus' desk, giving out instructions as if he'd been left in charge of the day staff at the club. The team at *Club CyEmp2*, the second club location had also mentioned the same, that Bruno showed up flexing. He didn't know what was causing the sudden assertion on Bruno's part, but Jason didn't want to bother Cyrus with it at the moment as he dealt with issues around his daughter, something Bruno had not been told about.

"What's up, Bruno," Jason said, sliding further under the desk to be sure the gun in his lap couldn't be seen. He watched as Bruno walked over to the leather sofa and took a seat, planting his feet, open legged on the floor.

"Came by to see what was going on. I noticed the boss has been disappearing a lot lately and only you seem to know what's going on. I've tried calling him and he's not answering. He doesn't usually do big deals out of state without me and it's odd for him to not include me in on what's happening. I figured I'd check with you for the latest. I also wanted to let him know that I took care of that matter for him with that guy who hurt that little girl. Trust me when I say he won't be using either arm or hands for years to come to hurt anybody else. I took care of business," Bruno boasted.

"I'll be sure to let Cyrus know."

"Let him know? What is that about? I can't talk to him myself? Y'all trying to cut me out? I've been around since day one with him taking care of his heavy-duty work and now I'm on a need to know basis and it's clear, there's something I don't need to know. I'm not liking how that feels," Bruno said.

"It's not like that. Cyrus has some things going on at the moment that are private. If you have work questions or business that you need direction on while he's gone, you can check with me," Jason said.

He liked the feeling of telling Bruno what to do, but by the look on Bruno's face, he was the only one getting enjoyment out of the moment.

"What's really going on? Is he out conducting new business? He making new connections? Oscar won't like that and he's already feeling the pinch with Cyrus not being available. There are some major shipments coming through and Oscar wants to introduce him to some new contacts out of New York who'll be another new connect. There is some really big paper to be made and Cyrus is off doing what now?" Bruno questioned.

Jason wasn't about to share anything with Bruno. It's true, he's been a game player from the beginning, but Cyrus had always warned him to watch his back when it came to Bruno. He always felt that once Bruno started making real money, he was going to want more whether it was with Cyrus, through Cyrus or around Cyrus. Bruno was going to get his and from what he's been hearing the past couple of weeks, Bruno was planning something on the side. It didn't surprise him that it was Oscar who brought him up to speed on side conversations he'd been having with Bruno. Unbeknownst to Bruno, Oscar was still in the game with Cyrus and like Cyrus, he didn't appreciate misplaced loyalty. For now, Cyrus told him to play along to see how far Bruno was willing to go to try and undercut all that Cyrus had built.

"Like I said, I'll get a message to him for you and he'll be back on Thursday, which is Thanksgiving. I understand he'll be unavailable that day also, but if there is a need for him, I'm sure a conversation can be arranged."

When Bruno laughed out loud, Jason held his composure, not backing down for even a second.

"You feeling pretty big sitting in that chair, huh? Are you sure you're ready to fill those big shoes and I do mean literally and figuratively? I know Cyrus is the man to learn from, but do you think you've learned enough to sit at the big boy desk?" Bruno asked snidely.

Jason finally laughed and leaned back in the chair.

"You mad he's leaning to me more than he's leaning to you? I'll let you assert what that means. If you have issues with leadership in his absence, perhaps I'll let him know you feel that way and see what he has to say about it," Jason noted.

"What, you trying to get tough? You channeling your inner Cyrus or something? Even on your best day, you could never be him, so stop trying. You're missing the balls that are needed to handle men like Oscar and the other players. These guys will spit you out and burn your body alive. I'm not sure they respect you the way they respect Cyrus, something the Boss should have thought about before handing the reigns to you. I guess he doesn't care if business suffers while he's off doing whatever it is that he's doing that's such a big secret. I'm telling you, Oscar is losing his patience. He may pull out and find another connection and then what? Are you ready to defend that action with Cyrus? I doubt he'll keep you in charge for long after that," Bruno said.

"How do you know what Oscar is doing? All of a sudden, you're the ear that Oscar is speaking into or are you holding his attention by speaking into his ear? Either way, I've got things covered here, at the second location, at the supermarkets, the apartment building and at the money houses. You don't have to worry about what's going on," Jason explained.

"Yeah? What about the studio and the new offices for the entertainment company?" Bruno asked.

"Cyrus is handling that directly. He wants to keep that far away from the other businesses. That entertainment company and the studio are his baby and he wants us to be hands-off, so steer clear of that."

"Look at you putting your big boy panties on and handing out orders! Ah, I love it. I just hope it doesn't get you dead because you're trying to play with the big dogs, bringing a knife to a gun battle."

Jason chuckled loudly as he rocked back and forth in the chair. Little did Bruno know that he was all about bringing a gun when needed as his hand moved across the one in his lap. He loved being underestimated which mean fools like Bruno wouldn't see him coming.

"So, he is out of town?" Bruno asked.

"He's not available," Jason retorted.

"Okay, I thought I'd see if the story changed in the past few minutes, but I guess we're going to play this game. Oscar and his guys are heading this way. Should I ask your permission to deal with them or would you like to lead the way and I follow?" Bruno asked standing and turning his back.

Jason gripped his gun, ready to pull the trigger if need be. There was a time that he could trust Bruno with his life, but now, he got the vibe that Bruno would rather take his life than save it and he was ready for him. Cyrus knew his worth even if Bruno didn't.

"You go ahead and get things set up in the basement and I'll be down. I have a few things to look over and you can hit me up on the cell when you're ready for me. Anything else?" Jason asked, feeling powerful with his finger on the trigger, ready.

When Bruno turned back around, he relaxed his grip.

"Nah, I'm good. I got you. I'll let Oscar know what's going on."

Jason nodded.

"Good. As usual, set him up with a nice bottle and see if Diamond and Sassy are in VIP tonight. If so, send them down to keep Oscar and his men company until I get there," Jason instructed.

Before Bruno could respond, he focused his attention on the computer screen in front of him, Bruno's signal that the conversation was over. He watched as Bruno, without another word, walked toward the door, shaking his head and humming the theme from the show *Power* as he left out. There was an underlying meaning and Jason knew what it was. They were at war, though neither spoke it. He was ready for it. The minute the door closed, he picked up his cell and dialed Cyrus. He knew Cyrus was heading back from Virginia that night, Thanksgiving Eve after spending the entire day with his daughter in Virginia. He wanted him to know what was going on.

"Hey, Boss. How was dinner?" he asked when Cyrus answered.

"Man, it was perfect! I love Ms. Rose. Besides dinner, she actually let the parents bake cookies with the kids. I have court next week and I can't wait to see what the judge says about the progress Shiloh has been making. I know you didn't call me to hear about all this," he said.

"Actually, I did. I know what having Shiloh means to you and I'm interested in how things are going, so tell me, bro," Jason said. "Business can wait until the end of the conversation," he added.

"Okay. I arrived with green beans and sweet potatoes that Shamari made extra for me to take. Ms. Rose has four other kids and some of the other parents showed up like I did. Shiloh was waiting at the door for me in this pink and white dress that I bought her. Her hair was cute and when I walked in the door, she asked me if I like her hair. She walked around holding my hand the hold time as if she didn't want to let go. We played games, watch television, baked cookies and then had dinner. After that, we had dessert and Shiloh showed me her room. I read to her and she fell asleep in my lap. I had the best time and don't laugh at how domesticated I sound. I'm loving every second of it. I know I've been slacking when it comes to business," he admitted.

"Yeah, but with good reason and things are going fine. When is court?" Jason asked.

"Next week," Cyrus answered.

"Is that the day you get your answer?" Jason asked.

"No, it's just another preliminary hearing. This time my brother will be there along with my sister-in-law and their kids. Marcus is going to try and get at least one overnight visit. He doesn't think I'll be able to take her out of Virginia, but the hotel where I'm staying when I come here has two bedrooms, a full kitchen and everything. It would be perfect if I can get it. I've been doing my classes, going to my sessions and I've never missed one of my visits with Shiloh, as you know because I've been absent on the business front. Shamari has even helped me find a house in their neighborhood so that if the judge ever considers letting Shiloh come live with me, it's not at the condo where no child should be," Cyrus laughed.

"Right!" Jason chimed. "I'm glad things are going well. It's odd not having you around much and everyone is noticing, especially Bruno. Oscar was right when he said that Jason isn't loyal anymore. Of course, Bruno thinks Oscar is going along with his double talk, not knowing that Oscar is keeping us well aware of Bruno's doings. When are you going to address this with him? You sure you want to keep him this close for much longer?" Jason asked.

"Man, I'm looking to make some major changes and he's already out. How far out he will be will be based on just how far he takes his scheming behind my back. Keep doing what you're doing and let's get together on Saturday at the recording studio, telling now one that's where we'll be. I'm having dinner with my brother and his family tomorrow and I'd rather not be disturbed. Ms. Rose is going to let Shiloh call me tomorrow and she'll get to talk to her cousins, aunt and uncle. They haven't been able to meet her yet, but we're hoping after the next court date, that the judge will allow that," he explained.

"Hey, you know I'm there if you need and want me to be. I know we're all about business, but you're the only brother I've ever had and I want to be there for you like you've always been there for me," Jason offered.

"I appreciate that and yeah, you're family. You should be there too. I'll give you the date and time when we meet on Saturday. In the meantime, keep your eye on Bruno. I'm glad Oscar knows to not trust him," Cyrus said.

"Oscar is a lot like you. He trusts those who are loyal to those who are loyal to them. He knows what you've done for Bruno and if Bruno is willing to stab you in the back, Oscar knows he could never trust him. I'll keep you posted. If you need me, call me. I'm getting a text from Bruno that Oscar and his men have arrived. I'll hit you later," Jason said and hung up.

Standing, Jason was glad he knew which side of the bread his butter was on. Too bad Bruno didn't and though, for years, he had been the person Cyrus went to when he needed a matter handled, he knew Bruno wouldn't be ready for him now being the matter that Cyrus would be handling.

Heading to the meeting, Jason walked toward the office door and hummed the theme to the television show *Power*, just as Bruno had. Too bad the song didn't mean the same to them both.

# 10

## *Next Court Date*

Cyrus sat in the front of the courtroom as they all waited for the judge to arrive. Beside him sat his brother and behind him sat Shamari, Mariah, Carmelo and to his surprise, with them sat Ms. Rose, Shiloh's foster mother. He watched her enter the courtroom and when she winked at him and blew him a kiss, she blew his mind by sitting alongside his family. Jason, sat toward the back of the room and remembering that, he turned around and told Jason to move closer. When Shamari made room for him next to her, Jason stood, straightened the tie around his neck that Cyrus knew had to be uncomfortable, but he was glad that Jason came dressed to impress. Along with the tie, Jason had actually purchased a brown suit with beige tie. Cyrus had never seen him dress up and realized he'd been underestimating his friend for a long time. He was now surer of some decisions he'd decided to make than he'd ever been.

As he looked across the room, Cyrus saw Daniella and the lawyer who represented Shiloh the first time. Like before, he was hoping to get a quick visit with Shiloh, who he knew was at the court. His missed his baby girl. His usual visit with her would have been today if it were not for court. He looked forward to each and every visit and she was talking more and more.

The night before Thanksgiving when he joined her for dinner, she actually talked most of the night telling him all about her school and her teacher and how much she loved writing her name in cursive, something he heard a lot of schools were doing away with. They went back and forth writing each other's names. He saw her hesitate once and he knew she was struggling with what to write as his name; was it daddy or was it Cyrus? He made it easy for her and spelled Cyrus out for her. She smiled and he knew it was fine that she hadn't asked about what to call him. For now, he was just happy she loved seeing him during their visit. She always had tons of pictures that she'd colored or drew for him that he could take back with him and he'd stopped at the store after each visit and bought more frames. In the new house that he was about to close on with Shamari's help, he would have plenty of wall space to hang every single one of her pictures. He couldn't wait for the day when he would be able to show them to her.

"Is it crazy that I'm this nervous?" Cyrus asked, tugging at his own tie, a first for him. He loved dressing in fine attire, but a tie wasn't one of those accessories he'd ever owned. Marcus had to tie it for him. He'd also helped him find a suit and dress shirt to go along with it. This time, he didn't wear any jewelry other than a watch on his wrist and it was bling-free. He'd gotten a shave and the curly black hair that he was letting grow out had been cut and his growing beard had been trimmed. He was ready and hoped his appearance was acceptable to the judge.

"It's normal that you're nervous, but we've got this. I saw the report the judge received on you and it's all good stuff. Don't be disappointed if this session is all talk and no real action. The judge is more focused on Shiloh's progress and visits with you than she is on you and you have family with you today and that matters," Marcus said.

"Yeah, the judge mentioned that. I'm sorry I didn't call you before that first court appearance. I'm also sorry about the time I spent staying away. I didn't realize How much I missed all of you, especially you. You've been my rock through this and I appreciate you, bro. You are going to love my baby girl," Cyrus said.

"Listen, my heart melted when I heard her little voice on the phone last week. The kids bought her some gifts which I have in the car. We'll make sure it's okay to give them to her. We can't wait until she is with us all the time in Maryland. I also love the house. Shamari sent me a link to it on-line. You've decided to buy that one? What's it like a few streets from us?" Marcus asked.

"It's exactly one mile from your house. The layout is similar, but a little smaller, though more in price, according to Shamari. I didn't care what it cost. I loved it and I know it's presumptuous of us, but I've asked her to go ahead and work on decorating it for me, especially a room for Shiloh. I don't know when it will happen, but I have faith that this judge will see my sincerity when it comes to my love for Shiloh. I love that little girl with everything in me," Cyrus admitted.

"That's good to know. I like this Cyrus that you've become. You're growing on me, bro," Marcus kidded.

Cyrus was about to respond when the bailiff moved to the center of the room and asked everyone to stand.

"Here we go," Cyrus whispered to Marcus.

"Yeah, and don't speak out of turn. I'm representing you today and unless the judge addresses you directly for a response, I speak for you. Clear?" Marcus asked quietly.

"I hear you. You're in charge," Cyrus quipped and looked toward the judge who entered the room and took her seat.

"You may all be seated," Judge Mathers said.

Cyrus leaned over to Marcus.

"She doesn't look as shrewd as she did the first time," he uttered.

"Shh," Marcus said back and Cyrus focused.

"Mr. Jackson, we meet again and this time I see you have representation and a few other people here with you today."

"Yes, ma'am," Cyrus responded and then looked to Marcus to be sure he should have responded. When Marcus nodded, he exhaled.

"Okay, well let's start with who you have with you today, starting with, who I assume is your attorney?" she asked.

Cyrus let Marcus speak this time and watched as Marcus stood.

"Yes. My name is Marcus Jackson and I am an attorney who is representing Cyrus Jackson today," he said.

"Same last name. Are you related?" the judge asked.

"Yes, your honor. I am Cyrus' brother and we also have family with us today. Behind us is my wife Shamari, my daughter Mariah and my son Carmelo. We also have Cyrus' best friend, Jason and you know Ms. Rose, Shiloh's foster mother who is here to also support not only Shiloh today, but also Cyrus."

"Well, well, Mr. Jackson. You do have family. Who is the lady who just entered and is now sitting in the row behind your family?" the judge asked.

Cyrus turned along with everyone else in the courtroom and his breath was taken away when he saw his mother sitting behind Shamari, who he knew had to be the person who called her. He'd been thinking about contacting his mother to tell her about Shiloh, but each time he tried to call, he couldn't follow through. He'd pretty much let her know that he didn't want anything to do with her, but that was in the past. His life was different in just a few short months and though he hadn't called her for support, she was there and that was all he needed.

"That's my mother," Cyrus inserted.

"Well, we have a full house of family and friends here to support you today, Mr. Jackson. This court is truly impressed in how that's progressed in a month. Now, let's get to the report and see what we have here," the judge said and opened the file in front of her.

Cyrus watched as she read while everyone waited in total silence before she removed her glasses and looked to the attorney who was representing Shiloh.

"Ms. Maddox, I've looked over the report, which I did earlier today and I just looked over this last sheet that was added to the folder just before I came. I see there is a recommendation from the state here, which I will read openly to the court in a few minutes. Thanks for providing that. I'm going to go over a few things before this court explains what's next. Does that work?" she asked.

"Yes, your honor," Shana Maddox responded.

"Okay. Mr. Jackson, I see that your visits with your daughter have gone extremely well. You were the first person she responded to and that was on the day of your first court appearance. I'm impressed by that. She seemed to take to you quickly, I see that you have made every visit on time and you've even completed the parenting classes and are still going to your own weekly counseling sessions. I understand that you enjoyed dinner with her the day before Thanksgiving. Tell me how that went," she said.

Cyrus stood up.

"Well," he said.

"You may remain seated. We're going to be a little informal this go-round," the judge said, and Cyrus sat back down.

"Thank you. Well, I think it went well. We had been spending great time together reading, coloring and talking during my usual visits and that day, we played some games, we baked cookies and watched movies and I was able to put her to bed by reading two books to her before she fell asleep in my lap. We talk on the phone because Ms. Rose let's her call me anytime she asks and I always answer and talk as long as she wants to talk. I love Shiloh so much. I never though anyone could make me feel love like that. Every time I hear her voice or see her face, I smile at the world because she makes it all better for me. I bought her a pink dress and she wore it for that dinner. She was so proud of herself and how pretty she looked. She smiled all day. I was sad when I had to leave and go back home, but I'm thankful that the court has allowed me all of the time I've been able to spend and bond with her," he explained.

Cyrus wanted to say a lot more, but wasn't sure he should.

"I've heard some wonderful things about you from a lot of people, especially Shiloh's foster mother. I've had Ms. Rose before me plenty of times with other families with cases and I must say that this is the first time that I've seen her sit in support of a family. Her glowing recommendation of you is the best I've ever seen and I've grown to trust her opinion greatly. Shiloh's case worker has been in your corner from the beginning and I've been told that she's never wrong in her assessment of a parent and she believes that Shiloh would thrive under your care and love. I have letters here from your niece, nephew, sister-in-law, your brother and even one I received from your mother just this morning before I came into my chamber. There are a lot of people in your corner pulling for you and Shiloh to succeed. I understand that you're in the process of closing on a new home and that's taking place on Friday of this week. Is that correct?" she asked.

"Yes, it is. I'm moving into a home close to my brother and his family so that if the court decides that

I can have a chance to raise my daughter, I want to do it around family who will be there to support. I've also looked into the schools in that area and other activities that I could enroll Shiloh in and be involved in with her like dance classes, gymnastics and art classes. She loves to draw," he joked.

"Yes, I heard about all the pictures the two of you draw and then exchange. Ms. Rose has shown pictures of the wall where Shiloh likes to hang the drawings you give her after your visits. I like that. Clearly she loves you and enjoys being around you."

"I love her very much. She's my life and I would do anything for her. I may not have known she existed, but now that I do, I can't imagine my life without her," he explained.

"How is business going? What are your hours?" she asked.

"My business partner, Jason, who is here today will be taking over running things, if and when I get Shiloh, so that I can focus on being a father to her. I will continue to run my entertainment company, which is a dream that I've had since I was a child who had fallen in love with music. We're going to be hiring extra staff to help take over the day to day that I would usually run, again, so that Shiloh can be my priority. This would be new for, not only me, but for Shiloh and I want to be sure that I'm providing an environment where she knows she's loved and wanted and where she can thrive," he admitted.

"I see you've learned a lot from your parenting classes," the judge said.

"Yes, they were very enlightening," Cyrus responded.

"Ms. Maddox, is there anything that you would like to add in before I discuss next steps?"

"Just that, and you have this in your papers, that the state of Virginia finds that Mr. Jackson would be a great father to Shiloh and when the judge finds that it's the right time to see how things will work out, we are in full agreement and will work with our Washington, D.C. office to make sure oversight continues until full custody is awarded, if that is the decision of the court," she responded.

"Thank you for that. So, Mr. Jackson, I've been watching your case pretty closely and have been asking for weekly records and everything came to me with a glowing recommendation. I have to say that I am truly impressed. As you remember, I wasn't too impressed with what I knew about you and what I saw in you during your first court appearance, but knowing who someone truly is isn't just about what's on paper or in a file, it's in their actions and you're shown this court that you are sincere in your desire to be a father to this little girl and I can see that you need her as much as she needs you," she said.

"That is true," Cyrus stated loudly, which caused the judge to laugh. He then laughed himself.

"Well, I would usually listen to both sides give

their insight of what the court should render as its decision, but I don't need to do that. Mr. Jackson, if I were to give you temporary custody, say for three months and then have you back here in court to check in with me on how things are going, what would you say?" she asked.

Without thinking, Cyrus stood up so fast, the chair behind him tumbled to the floor.

"Today?" he asked.

"Well, I can't do it today because there is a lot involved with moving a child from one Virginia to another jurisdiction. There is a lot that has to be put in place, but if I said in two weeks, you could pick your daughter up, just in time for the Christmas holiday season and spend the next couple of months bonding with her at home, at your home, would that work for you?" she asked.

"Yes! Oh, yes! From my heart, yes!" Cyrus screamed.

"Yes!" Mariah screamed behind him and everyone laughed.

"I guess you're ready to get to know your cousin," the judge said.

Cyrus winked at Mariah as she nodded her head yes.

"We all are. I love my daughter and I want her home with me, if that is okay with the court," Cyrus said.

"Mr. Cyrus, I'm going to go out on a limb and say

that it is okay with the court. Two weeks from today, you can pick Shiloh up from Ms. Rose's house and take her to Washington, D.C. with you for three months. We'll set a court date at that time and I expect to see you back here to discuss those thirty days. You'll have to make sure she's enrolled in school and get her records from her school here in Virginia. You'll have to make sure she has a Pediatrician, a Psychiatrist and a counselor. Ms. Rice will refer you to a D.C. caseworker and you will need to have your home inspected before Shiloh can move into it. I suspect none of those things will be an issue?" she asked.

"No, ma'am. None of that will be an issue. Two weeks from today? Thank you, thank you. Will I be able to see her today? I have my family here and they would love to see her, if they can," he asked.

"Yes, that will be fine. I'm sure Shiloh wants to see you and she'll love seeing all of her family. It will be nice to see your family again when you have to return to court," she said.

"We'll be here."

Cyrus turned around after his mother spoke. When their eyes locked, he knew the past was now in the past and his future would always include the woman who made the trip from North Carolina to stand with him in support of him being able to raise his daughter. They had to also get to know each other again, but he was ready for it. For Shiloh, he would put pride aside to make sure she had all of her family around her.

“Great. That’s my ruling. You can go see your daughter and the court clerk will get everything processed. I’ll see you in three months, Mr. Jackson. Good luck,” Judge Mathers said and Cyrus saluted her. He was too overwhelmed with thankfulness to say a word.

He was getting his daughter. Even though it was a temporary agreement, that was all he needed to prove he was ready. He and Shiloh needed each other and he was finally getting a chance to be better than he ever thought he could be. He was about to become a girl dad! He was going to be in her corner for anything she needed, wanted or wanted to become. He was all-in.

# 11

Bruno shot his gun off at the door of the old metal barn again out of frustration. He couldn't believe that Cyrus was pulling back from the business he helped him create and not only that, but he was giving Jason a full partnership in everything except for the entertainment company. He felt betrayed after the years he'd put in trying to prove himself to Cyrus. What did he get out of the deal? The opportunity to keep doing what he was already doing. He wouldn't stand for it. He had a trick or two up his sleeve and Cyrus would be sorry. Little did his boss know that he'd found out what had kept Cyrus so busy all these months. Jason didn't have to tell him about Cyrus' daughter. He had connections and a woman he was intimately involved with who worked for child services in D.C. called and told him that she'd come across a file to process that listed Cyrus as the father of a five-year-old little girl out of Virginia who had been orphaned when her mother died in a car crash.

"He thinks he's slick keeping me out of the loop, but he'll be sorry when I broker a new deal with Oscar, cutting Cyrus and Jason out of millions!" Bruno shouted and shot off his gun again.

"Hey, bro. Watch where you're shooting that."

Bruno forgot he had come out to shoot a few rounds in an open field with one of his street corner guys, someone he knew had his back.

"Yeah, whatever. I didn't put a bullet in you, so chill," he said.

"I got that you're pissed, but you can't say you didn't see this coming. For months, everyone had been talking about where is Cyrus? What's Cyrus been up to? Why isn't Cyrus around? We all had a feeling that whatever was going on, it involved him getting out of the drug and money laundering business. Have you ever known him to not be involved in the day-to-day operations of it all? Never! Not in the years that I've been your right-hand. Things were bound to change and he can afford to back out of it all. He's made millions over the years. He could live off of that and never have to get back in the game a day in his life," Tony said.

"Yeah, but that's only for him and Jason. What about everyone else? What about me? I'd like to have that kind of money," Bruno said, taking aim and firing again.

"Man, you have money," Tony said.

"I have money, but I don't have that kind of money and that's what I want. If Cyrus backs out, Jason can't hold things down. He's not ready for that. I was the one in the room with Cyrus for every deal he made. I was the one who had his back and doing all the runs. Do you know how many bodies are on my hands for him? He gave orders and I carried them out without questions. Now, this is how he treats me? Yeah, he'll get his. He'll get his for sure. That bastard is making all these changes for some kid he didn't even know he had. All of a sudden, everything has to change for her," Bruno said on a grunt before shooting his gun off again.

"Bruno, chill with the gun, man. You're killing my ears and though we're far out, someone may hear and call the cops and then what? You need to calm down. What are you going to do? You can't go up against Cyrus. I know you've been the muscle, but he's ruthless. He would kill you even if he knew you were thinking this way," Tony said.

"Yeah, right. He'd try. He's ruthless, but so am I. The difference is, I don't have a kid that I care about and it seems he's all loving and father-like now and that kid means more to him than this organization. Kids are a dime a dozen and they come and go. If he's not careful about his decision making, he may end up losing this one. He pops enough women, he can make another one," Bruno said and laughed as he tried to fix the perfect aim.

"Don't even joke like that," Tony said.

Bruno knew that he shouldn't, but this was Tony, the one person he could trust in the world like Cyrus had Jason.

"I'm saying, if Oscar knew that Cyrus backing out on some of these big deals that will also impact his money was over a kid, he would strike back in some way that would make Cyrus rethink backing away. Jason is a bum and can't bring in the kind of money and know how to hide it like Cyrus does. Cyrus is a genius. Jason is a toad who only knows how to lick Cyrus' boot and do what he says. He's not ready to take over, but I am," Bruno said.

"You are?" Tony asked.

"I am. I have no loyalties to anyone. My only loyalty is to the money. I need to find a way to make Oscar turn on Cyrus to make Cyrus come to his senses. Just because he has a kid doesn't mean he has to give this all up," Bruno suggested.

"How did you find out that Cyrus was giving it all up?" Tony asked.

Bruno stopped shooting and turned around, putting the safety on his gun. He moved to sit on an old log that had been cut down and left.

"He held a meeting last night with the top-level guys in the organization to let them know that he was out of the game. He didn't give much of an explanation and I assume it's because he didn't think he needed to give one. He explained how Jason was taking over everything, except for the entertainment company, which he would run himself with a new team and that there would be no illegal activity associated with it. He was turning all legit. He went around the room and gave marching orders to everyone and he left me out saying that I would do what I've always been doing. That pretty much means that I'm still the flunky," he said.

"Man, I could kill him and I'm mad enough to do it," Bruno said, kicking the dirt in front of him.

"Don't even put that out there."

"I won't have to because after what I tell Oscar, he'll do it. Did I tell you that three years ago, Cyrus killed one of Oscar's men? That's right. There was some question about what happened to the guy and Oscar was livid when the guys body had been found, burned to a crisp. That was all Cyrus, but no one knows but me and Jason. I think Oscar suspected Cyrus but it was never proven. I'm a witness and I'm going to bring it up to Oscar and also spring on him why Cyrus is backing out of every deal that would continue to bring in millions of dollars. Oscar will see my loyalty to him and hit back at Cyrus. I think he cherishes that kid too much. I wonder what he would do if something happened to her? You know they say, the answer to really hurting someone isn't in killing them – it's in killing someone close to them," he said.

"Are you crazy talking about hurting a kid? You

can't be that pissed," Tony exclaimed.

"He's messing with my money, so yeah, I can," Bruno said and pulled out his phone.

When the caller answered, he smiled.

"Oscar!" Bruno said, standing and walking toward the metal shed.

"What's up Bruno?" Oscar asked.

"I have some news for you about Cyrus that I don't think you'll like and I know what he's pulling out of the businesses that have made you millions on millions on millions. Can we meet?" he asked.

"When?"

"I'm heading to New York today. I can come to you. I want this conversation to be on your territory. There are too many ears here in D.C.," he said.

"Holler when you get here," Oscar said and hung up.

Bruno put his phone back in his pocket, took out his gun and fired into the shed.

"Feel like a trip to New York tonight?" Bruno asked Tony.

"Nah, I have those houses you asked me to hit up tonight and collect from. That's about money, so I'm sure you want me on that," Tony responded.

"Right. I forgot about that. I'll check with you in a few days. If Jason or anyone else asks about me, just tell them I had an emergency and went out of town. If Cyrus can disappear without explanation, I can to," he responded and again, shot his gun off.

Bruno was happy with himself that he was about to take charge of his own financial future, even if it meant tearing down Cyrus' organization and Cyrus in the process. He hated the power Cyrus had anyway. It was time for him to have his own power.

# 12

Cyrus tried to keep one eye on the road and one on Shiloh seated in the backseat, strapped into her booster seat. He'd never felt such excitement and nervousness at the same time. The ride from Virginia seemed longer than usual and was most likely due to how happy he was to finally have his little girl with him and out of the foster home. He had to admit that he had fallen in love with Ms. Rose who had looked after Shiloh as if she were her own granddaughter, but being given temporary custody until their next court day was the best day of his life. He knew he still had a lot of work to do, but being given a chance was all he'd wanted.

Thanks to Shamari, Shiloh's room at his new house was all ready for her. Shamari had worked in record time getting everything set up from painting to carpet to furniture, in record speed. Paying cash for his new home, he was able to go to settlement faster than expected, but it was done and he was ready for his new life in his new home.

Sparing no expense, though, Shamari had to remind him that having a child is not about spending the most money. He wanted things to be right. For Shiloh's room, he'd had her room decorated in shades of pink, white and purple along with a princess bed, toys, books and a closet full of clothes that he hoped Shiloh loved. He wasn't trying to impress her as much as he wanted her to feel comfortable and loved. He didn't care what her life was like before. They were both entering territory new for them and he wanted to make the best of it.

"Shiloh, are you hungry? We'll be home in a few minutes, but I'm not the best cook. I think your aunt Mari made us some food I could heat up, but I'm thinking about picking up a pizza or maybe some burgers we can eat at home," he said.

"I want pizza," she answered and cheered from the back seat.

Cyrus smiled, seeing her reading one of the books he'd put in the back seat for their ride home. Home, he thought. It had an entirely new meaning since he became a father. He finally understood how his brother made the right choices in life and continued to do so for his family – especially for his kids.

"Pizza it is," he said.

"Ms. Rose doesn't like pizza. What will she eat?"

Shiloh asked.

"Well, Ms. Rose won't be at our house. It will be me and you. You're going to live with me now – all the time. I'm really happy about that. Do you think you'll like that?" he asked.

"Yes. I like you."

Cyrus chuckled.

"I like you too. Guess what? In our new house, you'll have your own big, pretty room. I can't wait for you to see it. Aunt Mari fixed it up real nice for you. I needed some help because I wanted to make sure it was perfect for you."

"I like aunt Mari and uncle Marc and Riah and Melo. Will they be at our house? I talked to aunt Mari last night," she said.

"They won't live there, but they will come over a lot and we'll go to their house for visits too. You may see Riah and Melo at school. On Monday, you'll start a new school and they go there. Sometimes, aunt Mari may pick you up and take you to school with them," he said.

"What about granny?" she asked.

Cyrus looked back at her questioning who that was?

"Granny? Who is that?" he asked.

"She said I can call her Granny when we went to eat. You remember her?"

Cyrus thought about it and realized Shiloh was making reference to his mother who had come from

North Carolina and surprised him in court after Shamari called her and brought her up to date. He was shocked to hear that his mother had dropped everything and came to support him. Their relationship had always been tense, but things seemed different, especially after that day. He'd talked to his mother several times over the past two weeks. Enough years had passed that the reasons for his distance over the years had dissipated and the focus was on family.

"Oh, granny. She'll come to visit sometime. Everybody is looking forward to spending time with you," he said.

"You too?" Shiloh asked and when their eyes locked in the rearview mirror, Cyrus winked at her and smiled brighter when she smiled.

"Most of all me. I've been waiting a long time to be your dad. I'm new at this, but I'm going to try hard to be a good dad," he said.

"Do I call you dad?" Shiloh asked.

"Well, what do you want to call me?" he asked.

"Can I call you daddy? I hear other kids say that and it makes their dad smile. I like daddy," she exclaimed.

Cyrus had to shake off the feeling of tears welling up in his eyes. Who was he? There were emotions taking over him that he'd never felt before and hearing his daughter say she wanted to call him daddy almost took him out. He'd never felt so useful, so needed in his entire life. This is what it felt like to love a child with everything in you.

"I love that! I've never had anyone to call me daddy before and I love how it sounds."

"Okay, daddy," Shiloh said.

Cyrus grinned wide and made sure Shiloh could see it.

"See my smile! I love hearing you call me daddy. What do you like on your pizza? I'm going to order it and stop and pick it up on our way. I like cheese and pepperoni," he said.

"Me too. It's my favorite!"

"We like the same pizza? See, that's why we are daddy and Shiloh!"

"Yeah!" Shiloh sang out, causing him to rock with happiness in his seat.

Crossing the Woodrow Wilson bridge, Cyrus found a music station and hummed as they drove while his mind drifted to the life he lived before Shiloh and how he needed to make major changes. The kind of people he was involved with wouldn't usually let him back out of all the deals he'd been brokering for years and with the amount of money that floated between him and his suppliers, they were going to look for things to continue. He was happy he had a guy like Oscar in his corner whose only purpose was making sure he would continue to be a rich man. He told Oscar that he had faith in Jason and Oscar went with that. There was no way he could do it while looking after his daughter. If things went wrong, he could either lose her or put her life in danger. His biggest client, Oscar was a dangerous man, but so was he and the last thing he wanted was any kind of battle with him over loss money. They had spoken several times over the past few weeks and he was happy that they had reached a deal that worked on both sides.

Already, he had been getting messages from Jason that tension was rising because of how absent he'd been lately, but it couldn't be avoided. He has Shiloh and nothing was as important as her and he would not risk losing her for anything or anyone, not even the money he knows he'll be giving up. After his meeting with is organization, he knew there would be issues and he and Jason expected some stumbling blocks, but he trusted that Jason had learned a lot from him over the years and all would be fine. He looked at Shiloh in the backseat, enjoying her book and looking precious in the new pink and white winter coat he took with him when he left the night before to spend at a hotel in Virginia so that he could get her first thing in the morning without having to deal with Virginia traffic. His heart raced with so much love as he got out of his truck and saw her standing in the door waving at him, excited that he was coming to see her and this time, to pick her up to come and live with him.

While in the hotel the night before, he'd been anxious. He looked through the papers he'd been given from the new school Shiloh would be attending first thing Monday morning. The moment he got word that he was getting her, he went to the private school where his niece and nephew went and paid the tuition for the full year for Shiloh to attend. He also purchased the necessary uniforms, based on the sizes he'd been given from Ms. Rose. Shamari had gone with him to pick out Shiloh's school back pack and lunch bag and all of the school supplies she would need. He didn't want any down time for her going from one school to the next in order to keep her life as normal as possible. After the judge made her ruling he still had to wait two weeks before he could pick up Shiloh allowing everything to get through the system so that the records could be updated to reflect Shiloh's move from Virginia to D.C. He got word that he could pick Shiloh up on Saturday morning and on Friday evening, he took the ride to Virginia and after a sleepless night, he got up early and headed to the house.

Per the court requirement, he'd also secured a counselor for her and had already set up weekly Friday afternoon sessions, not just for Shiloh, but for the two of them together also. That wasn't required by the court, but after his sister-in-law recommended he give that a try, he was all for it. Being a father was new and though he was mentally preparing himself for making mistakes, he wanted to be able to think ahead of anything going wrong in order to head it off before it started.

His life was split between the life he wanted to have with Shiloh and the one he knew he needed to leave behind.

In the weeks that he'd been trying to stay on top of everything with Shiloh, he knew his business with his partners had been slacking. He'd put people on where he could to handle things, but people were used to working with him directly where having stand-ins didn't work for them. The one legitimate business that he didn't allow any illegality to flow through was his recording studio and his entertainment company where he would also be managing new talent. He'd always had an interest in the background of producing good music and he had four up and coming artists who were about to blow the R&B scene out of the water, bringing attention back to good, old sexy, romantic music with the likes of the days of Barry White and Luther Vandross. That was still good music and he was looking to tap into that. He also had a sister who grew up on music by Anita Baker and if people who heard her sing closed their eyes, that's who they would think they were listening too – that soft, sultry sound.

Finding some good music on the radio, he found a station that was playing an old Temptations song. When he heard Shiloh begin to sing it in the back seat, he turned it up and sang along with her. Until this moment, he didn't realize being a father was the greatest gift he could ever receive. Being a girl dad was even better!

**

"How do you think things are going at the house?" Shamari asked Marcus as he tried to cuddle up next to her in bed after making sure their kids were down for the night. She snuggled closer to him while she had trouble getting her mind to stay in the moment. Since she only had sisters, she never got the chance to experience what it was like to have a brother until she met and married Marcus and with that marriage came Cyrus. She loved him like a brother and wanted the best for him. Knowing what becoming a father now meant to him, she wanted everything to be perfect.

"Really, Mari? This is the first night in over a week that we're in bed at a decent hour either because of my late days at the firm or your change in schedule at the hospital. The kids are in bed early and I'm not tired and my plan was for you to put me to sleep in a hot, sexy way, but you want to talk about Cyrus," Marcus said and sat up straight in bed.

Shamari reached over and turned on the light on the nightstand and turned to him.

"I'm sorry, baby. I don't mean to ruin the moment and I promise you that it's not lost to us tonight. I'm just worried about how things are going."

"Well, he called us when he and Shiloh arrived to the house and he told you how happy she was to see her room. He said they brought pizza home and that he was going to let her have cereal in the morning.

You ran through the checklist for the night with him like a mother-hen and though I know he appreciated it, I need to make sure you allow him to figure some things out and not do everything for him. He has to learn just like any other parent would. He has to learn how to cook for her and not have you spending all your time preparing meals for him to heat up. He has to figure out laundry and no longer dry-clean everything they have. You already know that house is like Fort Knox and Shiloh is going to be safe. The street in him wouldn't have it any other way. He told me about the alarm system on the house and I'm afraid to go there thinking the property is booby-trapped," Marcus quipped.

Shamari punched him playfully on the arm.

"I know you're joking, but he needs us to help him. I want everything to be perfect. He still has to go back to court in a few months and we have to make sure Shiloh is still in one piece. Cyrus is used to worry about Cyrus only and now there's a little girl to think about. He has to do things differently. He told me about some of the things he's been involved in and I was shocked that he had that much going on both legally and illegally. Did he tell you about the kind of money he has? He paid cash for the house! He paid six-hundred thousand dollars in cash for a house and that was mere change to him. Did you know he had that kind of money?" she asked.

"Yes, he told me and with his new desire to go

straight, he's going to need it. I am an officer of the court, so I told him not to tell me anything other than what he needed to tell me, but I understand he's a millionaire several times over and he's done one hell of a job hiding it. I won't dive into that, but I will tell you that I made it clear to him that no amount of money will replace Shiloh if she's taken away from him for any reason, so he had better get on the straight path and do it soon. I think he wants to invest more of his money into the music business and really build up his entertainment company. I am going to help him with that by connecting him with some guys I've represented who I think can help him. We're going to help him do what needs to be done to get his life right, but that part of his life that's not on the up-and-up is going to interfere and could mean trouble for him. I can't help with that and neither can you. He's fine, right now. He and Shiloh are going to bond in that house and if he needs something, he'll call us."

Shamari huffed and crossed her arms across her chest as she leaned back against the two pillows behind her back.

"I know you're right. I just want so much for him. He's your brother and the only brother I've ever had. I have two sisters and having a brother is great. Though you and Cyrus have had your troubles, it's good to have him back in the fold with us and the kids can't stop talking about uncle Cyrus. We're a family again and now we have Shiloh. Did he tell you he's taking her to an event at the zoo tomorrow? It's for the upcoming Christmas holiday. I was given some tickets at work and I gave two to him. Our kids have been to the zoo plenty of times and Shiloh has never been. I thought it would be a great way for them to spend a Sunday by doing something fun before she starts school on Monday. I just want to know how their evening went after I talked to him. They were just about to eat. Did she like her new pajamas he bought for her to wear after her bath? Did he remember to tie her hair up? He sent me a picture of how Ms. Rose braided it up and it was really nice. Will he remember the ribbons for her hair tomorrow? Does he even know where the zoo is? What if she doesn't want cereal in the morning? She might want waffles or eggs or something else. You know your brother can't cook," Shamari stammered out and sucked her teeth when Marcus laughed out loud.

"I don't mean to laugh, but do you hear yourself? Cyrus is a grown-ass man. If he has to, he'll take her to get a waffle or some eggs. There are plenty of breakfast spots to take her to. You're worrying and you don't have to. You helped him find a nice house a few blocks from us so that we could help with Shiloh when needed. You helped him decorate and get all that cutesy girlie stuff little girls like. You said he did good picking out new clothes and buying what she needed for school. My mother sent a ton of outfits and pajamas for her. I won't even talk about the hit our bank account took with all you did for them and it's okay, but let Cyrus tell us what he needs us to do and we'll be there when he needs us. What's important, right now, is that he bond with Shiloh and discover what it's like to be a dad. I didn't tell you this, but he sent me a text around nine tonight and said that Shiloh had taken her bath, put on her pajamas and he was about to read a book to her. He said lunch of pizza went well and for dinner, they had take-out chicken which he'd had delivered. He had gone through what he needed for Monday for school for her to be sure he had everything on the list. He's fine," Marcus said.

"He's really doing this, huh?" Shamari asked.

"Yes, and don't think he won't need you. Trust me, he will be calling here frequently and we'll go over to his house to visit, they'll come here and everything will be fine. Shiloh has family now and Cyrus knows we're here. He's even building a better relationship with our mother and you know how major that is. My mom is even coming for a visit on Christmas Eve, staying a few days," he said.

"Is she staying with us? I need to get her room ready."

"I think so, but I need to confirm. We still have two more weeks until Christmas. I think she wants to stay with Cyrus. She wants to make up for lost time and to get to know Shiloh better. She and Cyrus have been talking and that's good. Oh, and Cyrus said he was taking Shiloh to pick out a Christmas tree and decorations next week. He's never bought a tree before. He's already figuring it out."

Shamari smiled and again snuggled close.

"I'm sorry for worrying. I don't want to be one of those people who think that Cyrus isn't the kind of person who should be a father. He encountered that enough from that judge and I'm sure there are those out in the world who judge him. I don't want to be like that. I just want to help him where I can. I love that little girl so much already. I did from the first time we saw her after the first court appearance where you represented him. When I saw her, I thought I was looking at Mariah's twin. It's crazy how much they look alike. You all have those light-colored eyes like your mother. I will try not to worry so much and give Cyrus some space," she uttered.

"That's all I'm saying. I love that you want to do more and be that safety blanket for him, but he has to figure it all out and he will. Now, how about seeing what I need right now," Marcus whispered and pulled her closer.

Shamari went into his arms after reaching to turn out the only light in the room. She put all thoughts of anything other than loving her husband out of her mind and prayed that Cyrus and Shiloh were bonding well.

# 13

Cyrus had checked the house one final time before heading upstairs to bed. Looking at his cell phone, which had been pinging with calls and texts all evening, he continued to ignore them, promising that his night would be about him being present at home and not worrying about Jason or Bruno or Oscar or anyone else that wasn't his daughter. The majority of the texts and calls were from Oscar, but for now, he quieted those and would deal with later. He had to focus on distancing himself from that life and building the new one he was trying to have with his daughter.

He and Shiloh ate a dinner of fried chicken and green beans, the chicken which he'd had delivered and the green beans from a dish Shamari had given him to freeze. He put the television in the family room on the Disney channel while he cleaned up the kitchen, washing dishes, something he'd never really done since he'd had a housekeeper who took care of that at his condo. For now, he didn't want anyone that wasn't family around Shiloh.

After television, he ran Shiloh a bath and helped her pick out pajamas. After tying up her hair, he told her he had a special place he was taking her to the next day. Letting her pick out two books from the many she now had on the mini bookshelf in her room, he read one and barely got past the first page of the other when he noticed she'd fallen asleep. He shifted from his seated position on the side of her bed, tucked her in tighter and after turning on the nightlight near the door of her bedroom, he pulled the door slightly and went back downstairs.

Going around the large house one last time, he checked and re-checked windows and doors, making sure the alarm system was working on all spots. He didn't have to be this worried about security at his condo because without a key and a code, no one was able to get onto his penthouse level to enter his place. This was his first time owning a home with so many windows and doors and he'd also never felt more vulnerable. What he didn't want was for Shiloh to live in a cocoon of fearing the unknown that he lived in because of the kind of life he lived. He still kept two weapons in the house, but made sure they were secure from his daughter knowing where they were and accessing them. Remembering his life and what it had been for years, warranted having them.

Feeling that all was well, he finally headed upstairs and was now relaxing in bed, surprised that he was in it and it was barely ten at night- a first for him. He was actually exhausted, probably coming down from the rush of finally getting his daughter out of the foster care situation and home where she belonged with him. He smiled, happy with himself that he'd passed every test and challenge that was thrown at him. Even the judge seemed surprise at the person she found he was when his daughter's life was on the line. He knew he had to impress her, but it wasn't her that he cared anything about. Everything he did, he did for Shiloh.

Relaxed in bed, Cyrus felt sleep about to overtake him and he turned out the bedroom light and in his sweat pants and tshirt, new sleep attire because he usually slept in the nude, he laid, half laying down and half sitting up with his head resting on two pillows, he thought about the fun day ahead of him and Shiloh, their first real outing without any watchful eyes on them. Going to the zoo would be a first for them both. Growing up, family trips weren't something his mother ever planned. When Shamari offered him the tickets and told him of all the activities Shiloh could enjoy, he jumped at the chance to take her there. He now had to get some sleep. Minutes after turning out the light and finding his comfort spot, Cyrus saw movement at his bedroom door. Knowing the alarm was intact, the movement could only be Shiloh. He waited to see if she would signal that something was wrong. He was about to reach for the light on the nightstand when he stopped moving, watching Shiloh enter his room and in the next second, he didn't see her. Where had she gone? Leaning up, as his eyes still adjusted to the dark, he didn't turn on a light to not frighten her. What he saw bothered him. Shiloh had come into his room and from his spot at the head of his bed, he could see her curl up in the corner of his room next to the dresser that ran the length of the wall beside the door. Waiting a few seconds to see what she was doing, he waited. When she didn't move, he finally got out of bed and turned on the soft light on the nightstand.

"Shiloh?" he questioned walking over to her and finding that she was looking up at him, still curled up on the floor.

"Sorry," she said almost on a whisper.

"Sorry? Sorry for what? Are you okay? Why are you on the floor? What's wrong?" he asked.

"I woke up and I was scared from a dream," she said, still not moving to sit up.

Cyrus walked over to her and slid down to the floor next to her.

"Okay. That's not a problem. I have bad dreams sometimes too. Why are you on the floor like this?" he asked.

"When I lived with mommy, she would let me come into her room when I was scared," she explained.

"But you're on the floor," he offered.

"Mommy never let me get in her bed. She didn't like that. She let me sleep on the floor if I was quiet."

Cyrus felt his chest clinch.

"The floor? Like this? With no bed?" he asked softly.

"Mommy would get angry if I was noisy and she woke up."

"Come here," Cyrus said and opened his arms to his daughter. When she sat up and moved into his arms on his lap, he held her close. "I don't ever want you to be afraid that I will be angry if you are noisy. You're five. You're supposed to be noisy. I also don't ever want you to sleep on the floor. If you're scared, you can call out to me and I'll come running or you can come into daddy's room and I'll let you sleep on the other side of my very big bed. You see how big that bed is? There is plenty of room and you never, ever have to sleep on the floor – not in your own house. The floor is not a comfortable place and it can get a little chilly, especially in the wintertime when it's cold outside. I want you to learn to love your bed and to be able to sleep in it and feel comfortable. How about I go into your room with you until you fall back to sleep. I promise I will stay right there with you until I know you're asleep. Will that make you feel better?" he asked as Shiloh nodded her head after laying it on his chest.

Smiling, he stood, lifting her up to his shoulder and walked to her room. Placing Shiloh back in her bed, he covered her up and kneeled down on the floor next to her bed.

"Hi, daddy," she said smiling over at him.

"Hi, baby girl. You're such a big girl sleeping in your bed. How about we get one of your bears to put in bed with you? Would you like that?" he asked.

"The blue one?" she asked.

"Okay, the blue one it is. Using the night light to see, Cyrus found the blue one he'd given her a few weeks ago sitting on the little pink bench at her bedroom window. Handing it to her and tucking it in with her, he laid his head on the side of her bed and caressed her back until her eyes began to close shut. Though kneeling was uncomfortable, he didn't care as long as Shiloh could feel his presence. He stayed that way for thirty minutes until he felt she was in a deep sleep. Standing, he walked across the soft pink carpet to the wood flooring in the hallway and then into his own room. This time, he left her bedroom door wide open.

After going back into his room, he had a hard time finding sleep. His mind was cloudy with the idea that Shiloh's mother would have her daughter sleeping on the floor in any room for any reason. If it was because there was a man in her bed, then he hated thinking that she would be more concerned about a man than her daughter. His heart broke the moment he heard her tell him that she'd slept on the floor before. He remembered hearing she'd done it at her foster home, but they thought nothing of it. He was bothered by it. He'd seen fear in lots of people before, but never in the eyes of a child. He saw it when Shiloh realized he knew she was in his room. She looked like she was scared to move as if he would demand she leave his room. What had her life really been like before? He already knew he was going to have to work hard to make sure Shiloh found a safe place with him and when she needed him, he would always make her first in all he did. He was glad he was still up and had not woken up in the morning to find her on the floor. If he had to sit next to her bed every night until she had good dreams instead of bad ones, he would do it. The key to their life together was in him being home with her.

He was upset with himself for not being there for Shiloh from birth, even though he had no control over that. He remembered his own childhood and how frightened he was on nights when his father stayed with them and he didn't know if he'd be woken up in the middle of the night for an impromptu beating. Reaching for his cell phone, he called Marcus and hoped he wasn't waking him.

"Hey, Marc. Did I wake you?" he asked.

"You did, but you can anytime you need to. What's up? Is everything okay?" he asked.

"Did I wake the family?" Cyrus asked.

"No, just me. Hold on while I go downstairs to talk. I don't want to wake Mari. She was already worried about you and would have an attack if she knew you were calling this late. Is Shiloh okay?" Marc asked.

Cyrus could hear him walking across the wood flooring and punched himself for waking him.

"She's fine, now. I was about to go to sleep in my room in the dark and I saw her shadow come in a crawl into a little ball on the floor in a corner. When I asked her about why, she said her mother would let her sleep on the floor in her room. Brenda wouldn't even let her get into bed with her. I wanted to cry and you know that's not me. What kind of a person does that? Who sets out to purposely harm a child?" he asked.

"Cy, I know you're angry, but think about this one fact – Shiloh is with you now and she no longer has to worry about Brenda or the life she lived with her mother. I'm guessing it wasn't all bad," Marcus asserted.

"Did I tell you that I was the one who claimed Brenda's body and had her brought back here to D.C. for burial? I was the only person at the gravesite, but no one had claimed her and I didn't want the day to come when Shiloh asked me about her mother and I would have to tell her that I didn't know where she was buried. When Shiloh's case worker told me about it, I called a funeral home and had her brought here. I got a really nice casket and headstone and had her buried so that one day, if Shiloh wants to visit her grave, she can. I still can't get over the fact that she didn't let me know I had a daughter. I could have helped with her," he said.

"Is that where your mind was back then? Do you think you would have been open and ready to be a father to Shiloh? I don't know. That was a tricky time for you. Don't go over what you would have or could have or even should have done about a situation you were not privy to. All you can do is start now and do the right thing for her and you're doing that. She's doing what she knows, but you're already showing her what love looks like and that she doesn't have to sleep on the floor or go without eating. Start new from now and don't look back," Marcus suggested.

"Even when it comes to my own life with my father? He terrorized me and I never forgot that. There were times when you went with your father for the weekend and my father would just go at me with whatever he could find. I could never remember why I made him so made. Mom would do the same thing to me and tell me she did it because I reminded her of my father and she hated him, yet she continued to invite him back into our house and into her bed and the abuse would get caught up in a continuous loop. Those were bad times and I knew how it made me feel. I don't want my daughter to feel what I feel as she grows up. I want only happy thoughts in her memory," Cyrus explained.

"Bro, you can't control that. Shiloh will remember what Shiloh will remember. Good or bad, you just need to be there for her and when she needs a hug, you give her that. When she needs to crawl in your bed at five-years-old from a nightmare, you hold her tight. When her first boyfriend breaks her heart, you don't go for your gun – you tell her that there are other boys and she's worthy of one who will treat her better than the last. Being a father means finding the good in every situation and letting her know that if she doesn't have another person in the world, she has her daddy. You're already a girl dad just like me. There is something special about our girls where we want to make all of their dreams come true. We want to show them how a girl and then one day, how a woman should be treated. We want them to be happy about their choices and come to us with any problem. We want their good and their bad and we want to make it all better. Do that and trust that you're on the right path. I'm here for whatever you need. Let go of your past and be that daddy that Shiloh needs to erase anything in her past that may haunt her in the present."

Cyrus exhaled loudly and relaxed back on his bed. He wasn't sure calling Marcus this late was the best idea and now he knew it was the greatest idea. He shook off his worry and realized, he was only in the beginning stages of fatherhood. He had a lot to learn and he and Shiloh would get through it together.

"Man, I love being a girl dad," Cyrus said.

"Wait until she starts doing dance classes and wanting to paint your toe nails and put ribbons in your hair. She'll want to have tea parties and just sit with you to watch a movie without talking. She'll find activities that she loves and you'll be in the wings cheering her on or maybe on the field coaching her team when she wants to play soccer or volleyball. That's what girl dad's do and you are well on your way. I heard about the zoo tomorrow. Are you ready for that?" Marcus asked.

"I sure am. I never been to the zoo either, so I'm looking forward to it. I don't want to keep you up much longer. I know you have church in the morning. I'll stop by after the zoo to let Shiloh see everyone. I love you, bro. I don't think I've ever said that, but I'm on a better path because of you and I thank you for being in my corner," Cyrus admitted.

"Cy, you're on a better path because you recognized that being a girl dad was more important than anything else you had going on in your life and I'm proud of you. See you tomorrow," Marcus said.

Cyrus hung up and got out of bed. He made one last check on Shiloh and found her sleeping soundly with her bear snuggled up close.

Going back into his own room, he finally found his place of comfort and a sense of peace. He went to be smiling.

# 14

Jason was on the phone early in the morning still trying to reach Cyrus. He'd finally stopped calling after realizing Cyrus had turned his phone off the night before. He knew Cyrus had gotten a new personal phone and said he would not share it with anyone, including him, but now he wished Cyrus had thought differently with the news he had to share. Dialing his phone again, using the only number he had, he was happy that this time the phone didn't go directly into voicemail.

"Jason, this had better be good. Do you know what time it is? I have to get up in a few hours and get Shiloh to her first day of school. What's up?" Cyrus asked.

"It's Bruno. Oscar has been trying to reach you," he said.

"Bruno? You're calling me this early with mess

involving Bruno? What's he done now," Cyrus asked. Checking the time on the clock on his nightstand, Cyrus knew that Jason's story had better be a good one at five in the morning.

"He drove to New York to meet with Oscar. He told Oscar that you were the one who killed his guy a few years ago and then burned the body and left it for Oscar and his men to find."

Cyrus shot straight up in bed.

"What?" he yelled, but not too loud so that he didn't wake Shiloh.

"You heard me. He really laid the story on thick by telling Oscar that you did it to teach Oscar's whole organization a lesson. Remember how pissed off Oscar was when he found the body? He was out for blood," Jason said.

"I didn't kill his guy. Bruno did and he did so without my direction. Apparently, he did it over some girl or something, but it had nothing to do with business. There was some Puerto Rican girl that Bruno was kicking it with and he found out that one of Oscar's guys was hitting her too. She was fattening her pockets from both of them. Bruno found out and confronted the guy, telling him to leave the girl alone. This guy told Bruno he would back off, but he didn't. Bruno followed her one night to a hotel in Baltimore City and found that she was spending the weekend with this guy. He literally followed them around the entire weekend. When she went back to D.C., Bruno follow the guy back to New York. He was obsessed. Once there, the guy stopped somewhere to take a piss on the side of a building and Bruno walked up to him and put a bullet in the back of his head. He then put the body in the man's car, drove it to some landfill and set the body on fire before then setting the entire car on fire. He then leaked where the body was and that's how Oscar found it. I didn't hear about it until much later. What's crazy is, Oscar told me he already knew and that was about a month after it went down. Whoever the check was, Bruno paid her a lot of money to tell him what she knew and she said that Bruno had threatened him and she thought she spotted Bruno following her that weekend in Baltimore. You know how big he is – he can't hide," Cyrus explained.

"Yeah, I know all of this and you know all of this, but Bruno didn't know. He went to Oscar talking about how you were going to ruin everybody's money by backing out and he was looking out for Oscar's interest. He wanted Oscar to trust him and bring him up in the game with you out of it," Jason said.

"Oscar told you all of this?" he asked.

"Some. Most of what I found out, I got from Tony, Bruno's right hand," Jason explained.

"Who? Tony Baker? Are you serious? Tony turned on Bruno and hit you off with that information?"

"He did because he said he believed in loyalty and when he saw that Bruno was turning on you after all you'd done for him over the years, he knew that he couldn't trust Bruno to have his back in anything. His trust went out the door, especially after Bruno talk and pretty much bragged about hurting Shiloh."

Cyrus stood up out of bed so fast, he became disoriented.

"What the hell are you talking about? What does he know about Shiloh and hurt her how?" Cyrus asked, now pacing around his room. If there was one thing he knew, he knew that Bruno could be vicious and he'd always watched his own back while giving Bruno orders but to hear that he breathed Shiloh's name out of his mouth had his thoughts turning to murderous intent.

"Tony mentioned he and Bruno went out shooting so that Bruno could release some steam after the meeting you had with the team. He blamed what he was able to find out about you having Shiloh on her. He knows some chick or something who works for child services who told him she saw something in her files about you. Bruno was going to use that to gain Oscar's trust and turn on you. He was even willing to remove Shiloh from the picture to get you back in line, according to Tony. He said that was the final straw for him and that's why he called me."

"I'll kill him! Do you hear me? Bruno is dead. I mean he is dead!" Cyrus breathed loudly and huffed through his frustration. He had to remember he had a five-year-old in the room across from his.

"Cy, calm down," Jason said.

"He's dead. I'm going to put a bullet between his eyes. He threatened my daughter. You know how I am about kids, especially my own. He's dead!"

Cyrus knew he was getting louder and moved from his bedroom to the hallway to see if he'd waken up Shiloh. Finding her still asleep in her bed, he closed her door all the way and went downstairs so that he could rant louder to release the frustration of letting anything get to him. He meant it when he said he would give his life for his child and if Bruno thought he was going to try and take Shiloh from him, he had better remember who he was dealing with.

"Cy, seriously bro, calm down. You don't have to do that."

"Like hell I don't. You know I can't let that go. He made a threat against my daughter. He's a dead man walking!" Cyrus yelled and went into the walk-in safe he had installed behind the wall in one of his first-floor closets. In that room, he kept his gun collection and had the perfect one for dealing with Bruno.

"Stop it and listen. If you're going for a gun, put it down and listen. Bruno is already dealt with. You don't have a care in the world to worry about and you know Shiloh is safe. Even if Oscar hadn't taken care of Bruno, I would have it if meant you and Shiloh would be safe. Back up from the ledge, bro. Put the gun away I know you went in search of and think about your daughter. Don't go back to being that ruthless guy. You're a, what did you call yourself, a girl dad now.

Your only concern is Shiloh, but I wanted you to know. Oscar has been trying to reach you to let you know that everything was good and he's still in full support of you living your life with your daughter. He told me he would do anything to protect you and taking care of Bruno was a parting gift to you. I talked to him last night and he said he has kids and wouldn't take anyone making a threat against them. He values loyalty and knew he would never find it in Bruno. He gave Bruno what he had been thinking of giving him for a long time. The only reason he didn't was because you had Bruno as a member of your organization. Once he realized that trust in Bruno was over as he tried to literally stab you in the back, he no longer saw a need for him. Move on and love on that little girl. I hope I'm still invited for Christmas Eve dinner at your house," Jason said.

Cyrus breathed easier, put the gun back and relocked the room with his fingerprint.

"Next time, lead with Bruno being gone and you would have saved me the stress of almost having a heart attack over lighting Bruno's life up!" Cyrus cheered.

"I will always have your back, no matter what. I know we've been in this game together for a long time, but who you are now, I wouldn't trade for anything. We'll always be boys," Jason said.

"Yes, we will and you better be here for Christmas Eve dinner. I'm having it catered and my entire family will be here, including some family from out of state. Tell Oscar I appreciate him, but I would appreciate if he cut ties. He can reach me through you, only if he needs to, and I suspect, he won't. You'll do fine running things," Cyrus said.

Jason smiled on his end of the phone. The trust between them could never be broken and the faith that Cyrus had in him was worth more than gold.

"I'm all over it. Catch you later, girl dad!" Jason hollered and hung up.

# 15

Cyrus was up earlier in the morning than he ever remembered doing since he was a kid living at home with his mother and brother. He was still riled up after his conversation with Jason and never did go back to sleep. Even though he considered himself, for the most part, to be a businessman, his idea of getting work done meant sleeping in late and staying up even later in the evening. Now that he had Shiloh to look out for, he knew he needed to adjust his schedule to match what her needs were and with today being her first day at school, he wanted to do what his sister-in-law said he should do, which was get up early and get ready for Shiloh's day before she got up.

Cyrus smiled knowing he'd seen six in the morning before, but not because he was up preparing to take his daughter to school. He was experiencing his new normal. Usually, he would be just getting home or just getting to sleep.

Heading back upstairs, he quickly checked on Shiloh again and was happy to see that she'd slept in her bed all night without him having to come in her room to sit with her after a nightmare like the first night they spent in the house together. He was still shocked after that first night of being unable to sleep and seeing her little silhouette come into his room and when he thought she would come over to him because she couldn't sleep or possibly because she wanted water, his heart had stopped beating for a second when he saw her curl up into a ball on the floor in the corner of his room. He never wanted to see that again, but thanks to his brother for the much-needed pep talk, he knew how to handle it and stay calm if it happened again.

Going back into his room, he checked his notes on his cell phone for the things he needed to do before waking Shiloh for school. He'd been tempted throughout the night to check on her, but didn't want his presence to keep her up if she was a light sleeper.

He rushed to change into his gray sweat pants and a gray and white shirt. Rushing into his connecting bathroom, he brushed his teeth and washed his face before heading to the kitchen to make Shiloh lunch and to pull out her favorite cereal for breakfast. Thanks to Shamari, once again, he had a refrigerator and cabinet full of things they were discovering she liked. He still found his new way of life to be unbelievable. He wondered what his old crew would think if they saw him standing at the island in his kitchen pulling out the makings to fill Shiloh's pink and white lunch bag with enough goodies to make her first day at her new school a positive experience.

"Hi."

Cyrus looked up to find Shiloh standing in the doorway between the kitchen and his family room, rubbing her eyes, still half asleep.

"Good morning. I was giving you a little more time to sleep before school."

He watched as she walked closer.

"I'm not sleepy," Shiloh said.

"Are you hungry? Do you want some cereal?" Cyrus asked.

When she shook her head yes, he reached for a bowl, milk, spoon and the sugary goodness he himself loved.

"Can I have juice?" she asked.

"Of course. Orange juice? Apple juice?" he asked.

"Apple," Shiloh replied.

"Sit at the table and I'll get your juice and fix your cereal. You have school today at your new school. I'm making your lunch and then after you eat, we have to get you dressed."

Shiloh shook her head as he handed her a cup of apple juice.

"Can I take my teddy bear?" she asked.

Cyrus knew she'd grown attached to the bear in

the few days that she'd been with him, but he didn't know if taking it to school would be allowed. He would have to ask her teacher in the hope that kindergarten children were allowed to bring toys of comfort with them, especially if they were new.

"I don't if you can, but why don't we put it in your backpack just in case you can. I'll ask your teacher when we get there. If you can't take it out, it will be with you, but in your backpack, okay?" he asked.

Again, he watched her shake her head yes as he placed her bowl of cereal in front of her. He waited and when she didn't start eating he didn't know what to do. Was she waiting on permission or did he pick the wrong cereal? He was about to ask what was wrong just as she looked up at him.

"Auntie Mari says pray," Shiloh said.

Cyrus forgot that. It's not something he ever did, but he knew his brother's family prayed over every meal and when they had stopped over their house after the zoo the day before, he remembered Shamari praying and telling Shiloh that she should pray over her food.

"Oh, I forgot."

Cyrus watched her close her eyes and lift her hands in prayer. He was about to find something to say and then he heard her little voice whisper a few words.

"Thank you for my food. Amen," she said.

"Amen," Cyrus repeated. He smiled at her as his

heart swelled even more. How had he not had this in his life before? Before him sat the most precious sight in the world.

“Is school every day?” Shiloh asked as he finished making her lunch.

“Well, it’s Monday through Friday and it’s all day. There’s no school on Saturday or Sunday.”

“I like school. Will Miss Connie be there?” she asked.

He knew he was talking about the teacher at her old school.

“No, this is a new school. You’ll have a new teacher.”

“I like Miss Connie. She gave me crayons so that I could draw.”

“I’m sure your new teacher will let you draw. I put new crayons in your backpack already. You also have pencils in a pencil box and a notebook.”

“I like my bag. It has a princess on it. I want to be a princess. They are pretty,” Shiloh said.

“You’re pretty.”

“Not like a princess. Mommy said I wasn’t,” she said.

Cyrus was stunned. He didn’t know how to respond to that. He had to do what Mari and Marcus said and gently pull Shiloh away from the life she led with her mother. He didn’t know what happened during that time, but right now, his focus would be on making sure Shiloh saw her best self.

"You are beautiful, Shiloh. I don't know what your mommy meant by that, but I know what I see and I see a beautiful princess when I see you. What do you say to going out this weekend and getting you a beautiful princess dress?"

Cyrus beamed when she bounced happily in her chair.

"Can I get a pink one or a yellow one?" she pleaded.

"You can get a pink and a yellow one, but you have to always say you are pretty because you are and you have to be good in your new school. Okay?" he asked.

"Yes!" Shiloh chimed.

Cyrus made a mental note to ask Shamari where he could take Shiloh to get a princess dress because he had no idea.

"Okay. Finish your breakfast and let's get you to school. Today is a big day for you and we don't want to be late.

"Will you pick me up? Sometimes mommy would forget and another lady would have to take me home," she said.

"I will take you to school every day and pick you up every day. If something happens and I can't, Auntie Mari will be there to pick you up. Your new teacher will never have to do that."

"Okay."

As he moved about the kitchen, Cyrus looked over

and saw a puzzled look on Shiloh's face as she looked over at him.

"What's wrong?" he asked.

"You're my daddy?" she asked.

Cyrus stopped what he was doing and joined her at the small round table in the kitchen, taking the seat across from her. She knew he was her daddy, but something else had to be bothering her. He knew they needed to talk it out at her pace.

"I am," he said.

"Not Shell?" she asked.

"Who is Shell?" he asked.

"Me and mommy lived with him."

Cyrus figured out that Shell was short for Shelton, the man who was Brenda's boyfriend and had died with her in the crash. He was the only father figure, though not a good one, in her life. He was hoping to learn more about the man and about Brenda and the life they led.

"No, he wasn't your daddy. He was your mommy's friend, but not your dad – that's me."

"Shell and mommy aren't coming back to take me home?" she asked.

"No. Remember you were told about the car accident. It was bad and mommy isn't coming back. You're going to live here with me," he explained.

"I'm glad. I miss mommy, but I didn't like our house. I like my new room. It's pretty. I like pink," she said and resumed eating.

Cyrus smiled, happy with himself and appreciated the help of his family. He'd gone so long without real contact with them that he was happy to know that though he had been stupid and distant from them for so long, when he needed his brother and his family, they were there.

"I'm glad you like it."

"I really like my bed. I didn't get out of it."

"I know. You were a big girl sleeping in there all night. If you wake up and you need me, though, you can always come into my room. Just don't sleep on the floor. You can crawl into my bed until you fall asleep or I can sleep in your room on the floor until you fall asleep," he said.

"How come you can sleep on the floor in my room?" she asked.

Cyrus laughed out loud at how brilliant she was. She thought of everything and she did so deeply.

"Well, your bed is way too small for daddy. I wouldn't fit," he said.

"You could sit in a chair," she said.

"Yes. Yes, I could and I may have to get a chair just in case you can't sleep. How is that?" he asked.

"You are tall."

Cyrus could tell she wanted to say something at the end, but when her mouth remained open and no additional words came out, he wondered what was next."

"Yes, I'm tall. I'm over six-feet tall."

"Will I be tall like you?" she asked.

"I don't know. We'll see as you get older and begin to grow more. You may not be tall, but you know what, you will always be pretty. You will always be the most beautiful girl in the world. I'm the luckiest daddy in the world and I love you, Shiloh. I love so very much!" he proclaimed.

She looked at him and held his glance.

"I love you too daddy. Can I tell my teacher that my daddy loves me?" she asked.

"Baby girl, you can tell the whole world. You can tell everyone you meet and all your new friends and everybody in our family and I'll tell them too. I'll tell them that I love my Shiloh and that I'm happy that my Shiloh loves me. How is that?" he asked.

"I like it. Can we play tea party like in that movie yesterday on the television? It was fun," Shiloh said.

"Uh, yeah. How do you play a tea party?" he asked.

"I don't know. Ask aunt Mari. She knows everything," Shiloh said as she ate.

Cyrus turned around to the sink and chuckled to himself. He didn't know how Shamari would feel about that comment, but he considered it the world's greatest compliment. Already, his daughter knew who to go to when she needed answers that he didn't have a clue about.

"Okay, we can ask aunt Mari and then we'll play tea party. We can play anything you want to play.

Finish eating while I make sure your clothes are ready. Stay here until I come back," he said.

Cyrus walked out of the kitchen and then came back in. When Shiloh looked at him, he saw that she was puzzled knowing he couldn't go and come back that fast.

"Daddy?" she asked.

Cyrus had to say it.

"I love you, Shiloh. I just wanted to say that again," he said and smiled.

"I love you too, daddy!"

## 16

### *May – Six Months Later*

Shiloh rode on Cyrus' shoulders as they laughed and giggled while walking into the doors of the Virginia courthouse where they were finally having their next day in court. Though the judge originally said that he would have to return in three months, the date kept getting extended as the judge was getting frequent updates from Shiloh's case worker and doctors and even from her teacher at school. Months later, he finally got a notice to appear and to bring Shiloh with him.

After putting her down on her feet in the cute yellow and white dress that he'd bought her just for today, he let her run through the security gate the moment she saw his family waiting for them at the end of the hallway. All he saw was a flash of yellow with long ponytails flapping as she ran and jumped into Shamari's waiting arms. He had to empty his pockets and wait for the guards to give him the okay to enter.

Though he had on a black suit, he wore a yellow shirt, the same shade as Shiloh's dress and a paisley tie that he let Shiloh pick out for him. When he looked up, the bow he had tied in the back of her dress had come apart.

"Your bow on your dress is loose," he said as he walked up to his family.

"I'll tie it," Shamari said.

"No, I have it. I've become an expert at bows on dresses. My baby girl loves these frilly dresses and I love buying them," Cyrus said stopping to tie it.

When he stood, he went around and hugged each family member separately. The hall was filled with family and friends who made the trip from some pretty faraway places. He hoped they would all fit in the small courtroom.

"Mom, glad to see you made it. How is the moving going?" he asked.

"I'm all packed," she responded.

Cyrus smiled, happy that his mother was moving to be closer to him and his brother and their families. He and Marcus, together, purchased her a small home of her own not far from them and they were excited about her being in range for frequent visits. The amount of money they'd spent over the past few months of bringing her back and forth from their home to hers was well spent, but they wanted their family closer.

"Good. The truck is on the way next week," Cyrus said.

"Thanks son," she said.

"And don't forget, you have a room at both of our houses and any time you want to spend the night, just bring your suit case," Cyrus quipped and Marcus nodded in agreement.

"This is some crowd today," Marcus said. "Who didn't you invite?" he asked.

"I told two people, Shiloh told two people and Shamari put it on social media, probably," he joked.

"Hey!" Shamari kidded and punched them both lightly on the shoulder.

"Sorry, sis. I'm just saying, look at all of these people. Judge Matters may think we're trying too hard," Cyrus said.

"Everybody here is being supportive of what you and Shiloh have. You have not only held up your end of the promise you made to make her life better, but she is a happy, glowing little girl who loves dance class and gymnastics," Shamari said.

"She asked me last week if she could play soccer because someone in her class is going to play. I looked it up and ended up signing up as one of the coaches. I know nothing about soccer, but I will learn before her first practice next weekend. How do you think today will go?" Cyrus asked Marcus and Shamari.

"It will all be fine," Marcus said. "I'm going to

check on how much longer we will be," he said and walked away with Shamari close behind as she wrangled their kids along with Shiloh who were laughing and playing.

Cyrus didn't want to tell anyone that he'd been up since the day before, unable to sleep. He'd gone back and forth into Shiloh's room a million times, not because she couldn't sleep, but because he was nervous about what the day in court would be.

He knew things had been going well since he brought her home back in December. She loved school and he'd gotten himself into a routine of getting her up, getting her breakfast and lunch made, taking her to school and then heading off to work in the office of his entertainment company which had already made a name for itself with the launch of his first talent on his roster whose songs sat at number one and number two on the R&B charts, shocking the entire entertainment industry. He came out of nowhere and was already making hits. His next new artist was already making waves as well. He made sure that at the end of the day, he let his team do what he was paying them to do so that he could get out in time to pick Shiloh up from school. He loved walking into the building to her classroom and having her launch herself into his arms the moment she saw him. Getting hugs and kisses from her are what made each day special. Another part of that day was seeing Shiloh's teacher, Macie Cooper, a woman he'd gotten close to over the past few months.

The first day he took Shiloh to school, he was surprised to walk into the room and see a woman he'd once asked out, but had turned him down because she knew the lifestyle he lived and she wasn't about that. She remembered him too and was surprised he had a daughter and that he was more domesticated than she could have imagined, especially when he showed up for every event she hosted for families and he even supplied the donuts for her daddy and daughter day with donuts and tea, though the kids had milk. When she asked for volunteers to read during story time, he had volunteered and she loved how engaging he was with his storytelling.

One day, he asked her out, again and this time, she didn't turn him down. They'd been a couple ever since and he loved that Shiloh liked her a lot too. She showed no favoritism to Shiloh in class, though when she visited them at his house, he was sometimes left out as her and Shiloh played some game or another.

He looked around the crowd that had gathered and wondered if Macie would have been able to get the day off from teaching to attend. He knew she wanted to be here for him and Shiloh, but he also knew her commitment to the kids in her class was important. Feeling a tap on his shoulder, he turned around and before him stood the second most beautiful girl in the world. He beamed and hugged her close.

"You made it," he said close to her ear.

"I wouldn't miss being able to support you and Shiloh. My teachers are covering for me, knowing what this day could mean for you and Shiloh. I was hoping I wouldn't be late and it looks like I made it. There are a lot of people here today. You're loved," she said.

"I feel the love," he said and leaned closer to her ear. "I love you," he whispered and then leaned back up to his full height. "I know this isn't the place, but I wanted you to know. I haven't said it before, but that doesn't mean I haven't felt it. I've felt a lot of new things this year and I'm learning to not hold back on how I feel. I wanted you to know how I feel about you," he said.

When Macie leaned up, he leaned down and gave her the sweet kiss he knew she wanted.

"I love you, too. You and Shiloh are everything to me. I'm glad we connected again. That first time was awful!" Macie laughed out loud.

"I know and I'm sorry that was ever me trying to buy you like you were property in order to get you to be interested in me. I'm glad to not be that person anymore," he said.

"So am I."

"We're up everybody. Let's go!" Marcus yelled to the crowd that was gathered.

Taking Macie by the hand and picking Shiloh up in his arms, Cyrus held his head high and walked into the courtroom already claiming what is for him, was for him and nobody could steal the joy that he's been living since the moment he found out he was a father. He didn't care what happened in court today because he already knew he was a winner because nothing could top him being a girl dad. He had heard the term one night on a late-night talk show where Kobe Bryant was the guest and he didn't know what the words meant then, but he does now and those words described him perfectly. He was a perfectly happy girl dad and he wouldn't change a thing.

# Epilogue

## Two Years Later

"And the winner for producer of the year is, Cyrus Jackson of CyRum Productions!"

As the crowd who were gathered in the Staples Center in Los Angeles, California stood to their feet and cheered, Cyrus picked up Shiloh who sat in the front row in the seat between him and his new bride, Macie and walked the steps to the stage to receive his award. He smiled and kissed Shiloh on the cheek, seeing how happy she was to be with him as he accepted his award. Word on the street was that no one was going to top him for getting the award this year at the nation's biggest award program where the best of the best were honored.

After launching the career of four of the country's top artists, he was riding the wave of people on top of his fame and doing it legitimately. He was free to live his life without looking over his shoulder and that's exactly what he was doing.

Walking to the microphone and holding Shiloh and one arm and his award in his other hand, he waited until the applause died down. He winked and blew a kiss at Macie who blew a kiss back and rubbed her belly where he knew her five-month pregnant belly was hidden by the Vera Wang designer gown she wore. His life couldn't be more perfect and it was all due to the little lady he held in his arms.

"Thank you to the Recording Academy and to those who voted for me. I'm honored and blessed to stand before to accept this award for producer of the year. I want to dedicate this award to my daughter, Shiloh Antonia Johnson-Jackson. Because of her, I am the man you see before you today. This guy you see now isn't who I have always been, but it's who I am most proud of, not because of this award, but because of the father that I have come to be and love being. For years, I didn't know I had a daughter and once I found out, I put my all into proving that I could change and be the man this little girl needed and what I found was she was what I needed – I just didn't know it back then. For months, a court held my future with her in its grip and then one day, I went to court with a small army behind me for support and five minutes in, the judge told me that I was given permanent custody and she was my daughter, something I already knew, but okay, I let the court have their say. I had to change a lot about myself to be who I knew my daughter needed me to be. She's beautiful, happy and she loves pretty dresses like this one she has on that matches the red in my tie. Her mother and I love her very much and because of her, she's made me a girl dad, a badge I wear proudly. I would not be here, doing what I'm doing when it comes to making hits while still coaching volleyball and soccer and taking her to dance classes and gymnastics classes. I do it not because I have to or because a court said I had to, but because this is what a girl dad does. He makes his daughter a priority. I also want to thank my wife for blessing me with another daughter in a few months. I look forward to a whole house full of little girls if that's what we have. I will love them all as much as I love Shiloh and my wife, Macie. Thank you again for this award and I dedicate it not just to my daughter for making me a girl dad, but I dedicate this to all girl dad's around the world. Thank you and God bless you!" Cyrus said as the crowd again jumped to their feet to applaud him.

As he walked off stage and hugged Shiloh tighter, he thought about how his life had changed over the years and he knew that there was a reason Shiloh entered his life when he did.

"You're the best girl dad ever, daddy!" Shiloh proclaimed and held him tight around the neck.

"I love you, Shiloh."

"I love you, daddy. You came for me, daddy."

Cyrus tried to hold back the tears that had already begun to fall down his cheeks. He thought back to the many conversations he and Shiloh had been having where he told her as much as he could about his absence in the early years of her life and how the moment he found out about her, he wanted nothing more than to be her father all the time. He never wanted to be without her and if it took him years to fix his life and prove that he was worthy to have her, he would. One thing he'd learned was that Shiloh was smart way beyond her years and her little heart forgave him for being absent and he promised her he would never be absent again. She was happy he came for her, but more than that, he was happy that the road to her happiness and his was meant to be. Everything fell into place the way it should have. Cyrus didn't know where his life would have led, perhaps to death, if he hadn't decided to put his little girl's welfare at the top of his priority list. Because of that, she had a life that all little girls should have and he had a life that he thought he could only dream about. Shiloh and Macie were making all of his dreams come true and his life was worth living.

Make sure you check out book 1 of the hit series, "When God Says Yes." Get it at www.cherylbarton.net

**Rescue Me**

Marissa Ballard is "Delilah" living a life of shame in the eyes of her family and finally, herself. She's lost faith, not believing in a way out of her current circumstance. She tried living according to rules that weren't meant for her because her immediate desires outweighed the vision of what her life could be if she had stayed faithful.

One day, Marissa was so far down in the dumps over where life had taken her that she hated who she had become, a woman who turned her back on her parents and her six-year-old daughter, Lacey, for a life with a man who demeaned and degraded her. Shame kept her from going back to her life in Philadelphia, instead opting to let a man use her for his own selfish desires, tricking her into believing what she felt from him was love. Finally, sick and tired of being sick and tired, she called out to the only help she remembered her parents telling her she should call on when she was in need, but even then, she didn't pause long enough to listen and know that her cry had been heard and her path to redemption was being newly paved.

Roman Hale spent a lifetime rescuing those in distress, but couldn't save the one woman who was the light of his life, his dying wife. His heart was about to give up on a life of service until the revelation of a new purpose and a new love shocked him into belief. Roman wasn't sure his heart was as open as it once was and just when he thought about giving up on being that lifeline to the less fortunate, his eyes were opened to the reality that one great love in life would not be his only love.

Now Available, **"Release Me"**, book 2 in the series, "When God Says Yes". Get it at www.cherylbarton.net

Raynard: I heard you can sing.
Zoe: Like you've never heard before.
Raynard: Show me and I'll make you a star.
Zoe: Sit back, listen and then get your check book ready.

Zoe Hamilton had no idea that those words to music executive, Raynard Black, would come back to haunt her in her quest to use her melodious voice for more than singing in church. She wanted to be a star and was willing to sacrifice her dignity and the love and advice of her family in order to achieve it.

Jason Minor is a gospel recording artist on the rise and the moment he encountered Zoe, he knew there was more to her than her new, flashy lifestyle and the entourage who were paid to cater to her every desire to draw her in.

Zoe's instant friendship with Jason had her taking a hard look at herself and who she'd become as she finally discovered her true worth. Her struggle for release from her flashy, yet demoralized existence left her fighting to get control not only of her career, but of her life.

Raynard Black had plans that did not include letting his soon to be money-maker go and Zoe had to show him that her release would not be his doing, but that faith in the ONE who gave her the talent that Raynard coveted was the only source for escape that she would need to get back to who she was always meant to be.

*Make sure you check out book 1, of "The Brothers of Chi-Town", I Can't Let Go – now available for download and in paperback.*

## I Can't Let Go

Carter Garrison vowed to love, honor and cherish his wife, Sienna, forsaking all others, something he forgot to do during a weekend of fun, bad company and poor judgement.

Sienna Garrison never dreamed her college sweetheart, Carter, whom she pledged her life to, would break her heart and when he did, she moved out and moved on - or tried to.

What better occasion is there than a friend's wedding to stir up old feelings and memories of love, intense passion and nights of sensual titillation. Gazes from across a room after almost two years apart revealed depths of love that had never died.

Seeing Sienna again reminded Carter of what he'd lost and hc vowed to never let go by doing whatever he could to get his wife back even if it included begging and pleading. Is Sienna ready to forgive and take a chance on life again with the only man she'd ever really loved?

When Carter brings on the charm and turns up the heat, no woman is immune, especially Sienna.

*Don't forget to snag your copy of book 2, Swagger and Baggage, in "The Brothers of Chi-Town" series – now available.*

**Swagger and Baggage**

It's not a coincidence that casino owner, Torrence Allen, ran into his college sweetheart, Reese Michaels again; it's fate. As his memories unfold, he had tried everything to keep her in his life and his bed back then and failed at both. She wasn't ready for him then, but he hopes she is ready for him now.

Reese Michaels never thought she'd see Torrence again. Their split in college was dramatic and hurtful and still, no man had been able to win her heart. She considered herself the permanent third wheel to friends who had found love and marriage.

Their whirlwind affair, quickly turned into love just as it suddenly crashed and burned when a woman shows up to claim Torrence as hers. When it's also revealed that this woman isn't the only 'other woman', Reese finds herself left with a broken heart, shattered love and dreams of forever beyond her reach. How did she not know about the other part of Torrence's active and amorous life?

Torrence isn't ready to give up on having Reese in his life after his deceit. He finds himself in the fight of his

life to finally have the love and commitment he wanted only with her. His swagger had always won women over, but it's his baggage that's causing his life to spiral out of control and he could once again find himself without the woman he has always loved.

*Pick up, book 3, of "The Brothers of Chi-Town" series, Claiming His Child – now available for download and in paperback.*

**Claiming His Child**

Business magnate Dexter Patterson refused to let anything keep him from checking off all of the boxes equating to achievement in life to prove that though he came from a rough childhood on the south side of Chicago, he still thrived and became a success. Looking around at those closest to him, Dexter found that he was still missing something...Love.

When aspiring model, Alyssa Kincaid met Dexter, she couldn't get enough of his sexual magnetism, fiery nights of passion, and secret rendezvous. She thought they were headed toward forever when a surprising call from him ended what they had causing her to leave Chicago, taking with her a secret.

Dexter thought that no woman could ever tame him, not even Alyssa who entranced him with her sexy body, smoky, sultry voice and untamed desire. Too little, too late, he realized he'd made a mistake by walking away and then she was gone.

Time and distance didn't diminish the chemistry between them and the child Alyssa carried and never told him about had him in the fight of his life to win back her heart and the chance to have the family he'd always wanted.

Will Alyssa continue to curse kismet when Dexter suddenly reappears in her life or will she believe that his yearning for her isn't just because of their child, but because when she left Chicago, she took his heart with her?

*Now available – New Release*
*Book 3, "Heartbreaker" of "A Lovers" Heart Series*

**Heartbreaker**

In book 3, of "A Lovers' Heart" steamy romance series, Cameron Lymon, the sexy, youngest brother of Hollywood heartthrob, Cade Weston and Navy SEAL, Calvin Lymon, with his Master's degree in Journalism and a minor in Communications and Sports Management in hand, landed his dream job in Denver, Colorado as the co-host for a new morning talk show. Women love to call him the "Heartbreaker" because of the bevy of beautiful ladies he's left in his wake, not interested in giving up being a bachelor for falling in love. He enjoys taking after his big brother's old lifestyle of being a playboy.

Dakota Kane sacrificed a personal life and fought hard in her career to be the lead personality on Denver's top television morning show, but she was about to risk it all for passionate, steamy encounters with her new, much younger co-host, who is ten years younger and fifty shades hotter than any man she'd ever encountered. All he had to do was smile at her and she was a goner.

Cameron didn't know what he was in for when what he thought would be casual, behind closed door romps with the ever-so-sexy Dakota began to turn

into much more when his heart became as invested in her as much as his body had. As things turned serious, his heartbreaker status came back to haunt him and his relationship with Dakota was threatened by his past.

Cameron and Dakota have to decide if what they are

beginning to feel for each other is worth the risk of their careers when their secret love affair becomes the topic of public opinion and ridicule.

# About the Author

Cheryl Barton lives in Maryland and in her spare time she loves to read espionage, crime and romance novels, cook, watch Sci-fi movies, spend time with family and friends and enjoy Maryland steamed crabs. Cheryl is celebrating 30 years as a government employee and loves writing romance novels when she's not working. Cheryl is the author of 31 romance novels, 3 inspirational novels and is proud of 4 book compilation projects with several other incredible women called, "One Sister Away: Encouraging Words from One Sister to Another" – a series of books meant to encourage, empower and inspire other women. People often ask Cheryl which book is her favorite of all of those she's written. While she finds it hard to select one favorite, Cheryl still looks to her first novel, Bachelor Not for Sale, if she had to pick a favorite because it was her first novel and the one that inspired her to continue writing.

Cheryl was a 2018 Finalist of the Literary Trailblazer of the Year award, given by the Indie Author Legacy Awards' yearly event. Cheryl is a member of the Romance Writers of America – National Chapter and the Maryland Romance Writers and the Black Writers' Guild of Maryland.

Indulge in more romance and inspirational novels by visiting her website at www.cherylbarton.net.

www.ingramcontent.com/pod-product-compliance
Lightning Source LLC
Chambersburg PA
CBHW022123080426
42734CB00006B/235

* 9 7 8 1 9 4 8 9 5 0 2 0 6 *